RAJASTHAN

And from black cedars a lone peacock cries
Laurence Binyon

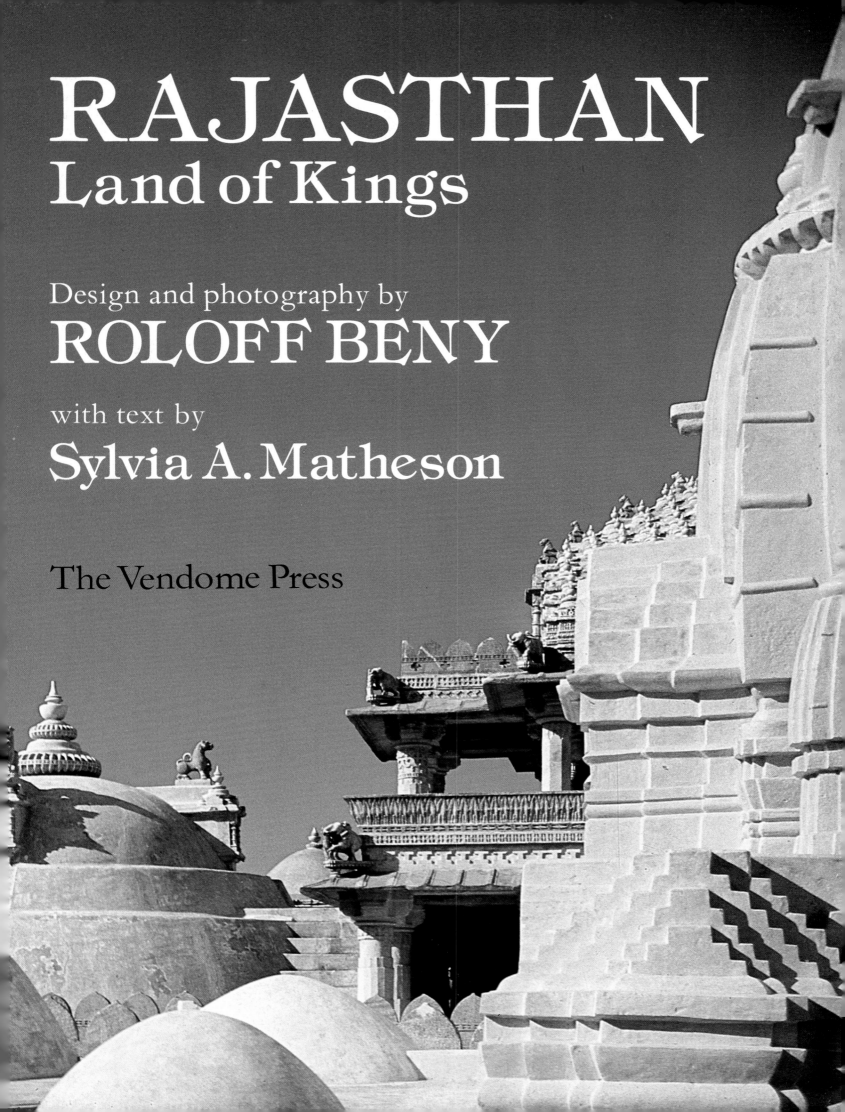

RAJASTHAN
Land of Kings

Design and photography by
ROLOFF BENY

with text by
Sylvia A. Matheson

The Vendome Press

CONTENTS

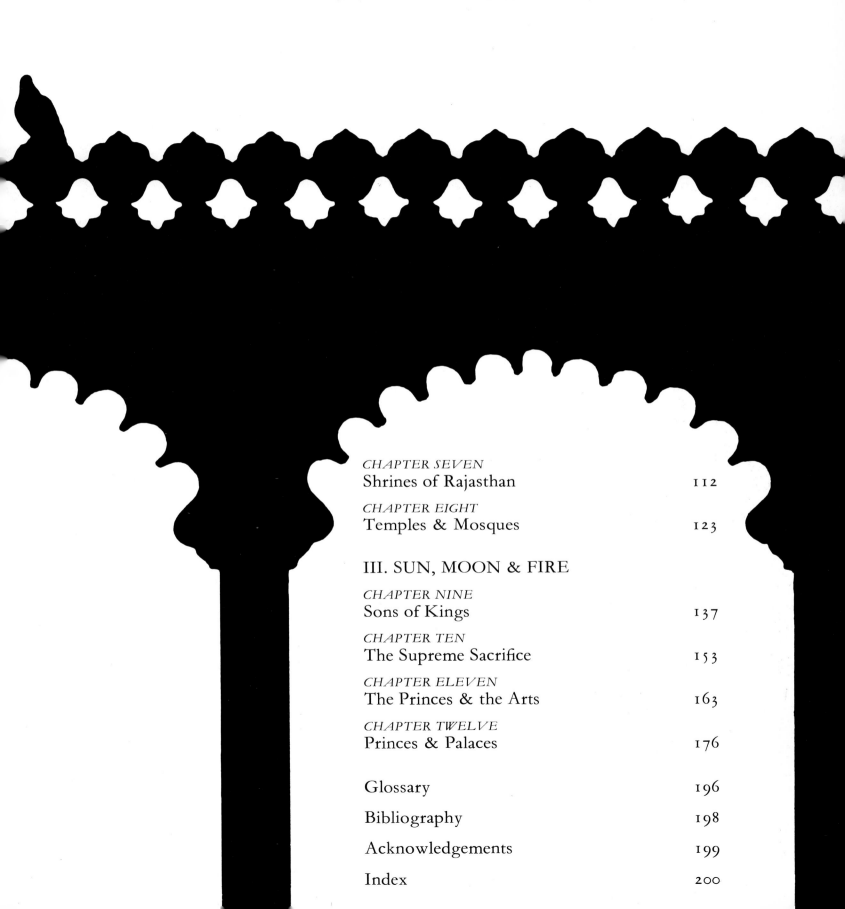

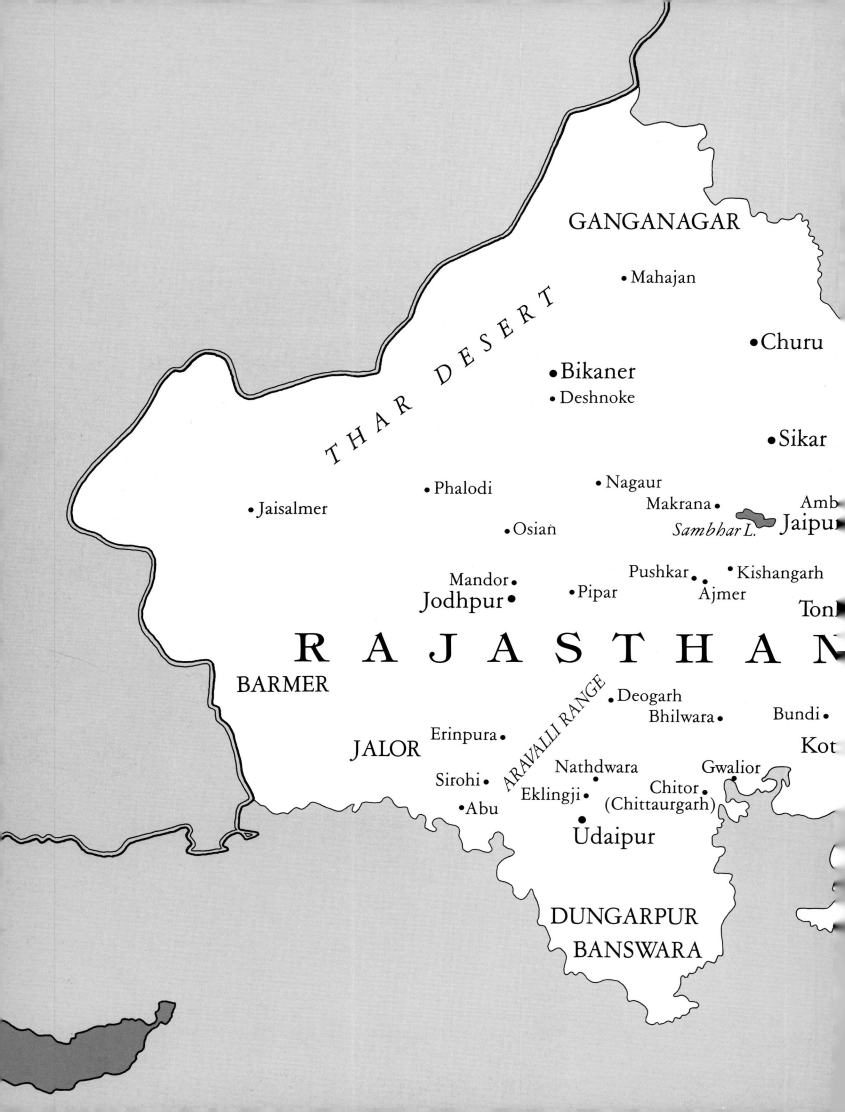

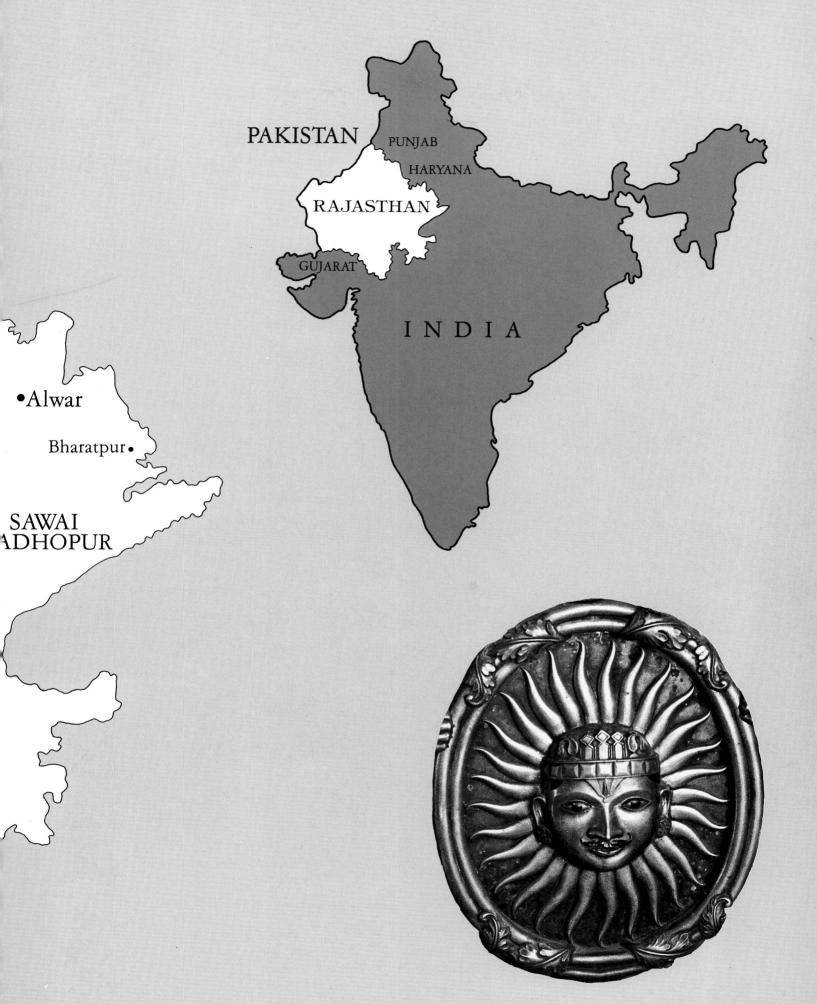

Preface

The Tigers of wrath are wiser than the horses of instruction.
William Blake

The life in even the humblest village of Rajasthan is worth a visual essay. Indeed, in India every region could command a book in itself. The name of India alone is a resounding one, conjuring endless vistas of imagery, as rich in meaning as the imagination can encompass.

My first exploration in 1963 overpowered me and almost obliterated any desire to return, so vivid was the human encounter, so fragile yet tenacious the ability of human beings just to survive. I was there in search of ruined cities, palaces, fortresses and paradises around the world for my book PLEASURE OF RUINS, inspired by the evocative text of Dame Rose Macaulay. I swore never to return, but I overcame my timorousness and ultimately travelled more than twenty thousand miles of Indian terrain from the Himalayas to beyond the Tropic of Capricorn. That became a book entitled simply INDIA.

One state alone, Rajasthan, obsessed me and drew me back. What drew me back: the taste of the mango fruit, the beauty of the white lotus, the screeching of peacocks, the sacred cow-dung plastered on trees and mud houses; the psychedelic colours of the bejewelled women drifting across oceans of sand, the luxuriously turbaned spare elegant men decorating the villages and the landscape – all walking with matchless grace. In every temple of white marble or golden alabaster, dedicated to the monkey, the sacred cow, the lowly rat, even a tree, I found jasmine and marigold, sandalwood and honey ritualistically offered to the gods. The myriad royal palaces and fortresses were often derelict, mere ghosts of a splendour rivalling the ornate courts of Europe's Golden Age.

How could I resist? I drifted through all this in an euphoric daze. The images, mystical and magic, simple and intricate, were not posed – they are, curiously, the real Rajasthan, and this is my humble tribute to a remarkable culture.

ROLOFF BENY
Tiber Terrace, Rome
February 1984

3 Detail of the lion and sun from the royal howdah in the City Palace, Jaipur

PROLOGUE
Land of the Dancing Peacock

If any part of a land strewn
with dead men's bones,
has a special claim to distinction,
Rajputana, as the cockpit of India,
stands first . . .
Rudyard Kipling, *From Sea to Sea*

Its official name is perhaps even more romantic: Rajasthan, 'Abode of Kings', which it was until December 1971, when the status of the hereditary maharajas was abolished. But nothing can destroy the heritage which the princes left to their harsh, beloved land of burning sun and shady forests, a heritage of magnificent palaces, massive, fortified hilltop cities and splendidly endowed temples. Reflected in the scorched stones of deserted castles and the marble monuments to Rajput heroes and heroines are unforgettable deeds of chivalry, courage and sacrifice.

No less than twenty-two princely states, together with Ajmer, were merged into present-day Rajasthan: states whose rulers claim descent from the sun, the moon or the sacred fire of Agni.

With such a background, it seems only natural to wake to the cat-like screeching of peacocks dancing on the dewy lawn, their exquisite tail-feathers raised in a shimmering halo, catching the first rays of the sun slanting through the mango trees. Peacocks, the most royal of birds, and the vehicle used by Saraswati, goddess of music, the arts and literature, appear everywhere in Rajasthan, enjoying the freedom of temples, palaces, meadows and markets, and depicted on coats of arms, castle porticoes and temple walls.

Known in Kipling's time as Rajputana, larger than Holland and Belgium combined, the state lies in the north-west of India, bordering Pakistan and the Punjab; almost touching Delhi to the north-east, a little further south it comes very close to Agra. Next it borders another former princely state, Gwalior, which was part of Rajasthan centuries ago. South of Gwalior lies Bhopal, which was a Muslim state amid the Hindu majority; then the southern borders of Rajasthan touch Madhya Pradesh and Gujarat.

The north-western area of Rajasthan forms part of the great Thar Desert, which engulfs Pakistan and is a section of the earth's desert belt stretching from Arizona in the United States to the Sahara, Arabia and north-eastward to the Gobi Desert of Central Asia. During a recent twelve-year period of

4 In the courtyard of the Gulab Dasji ki Baghichi Mandir, famous healing shrine at Sikar, a young peacock and a calf find sanctuary

drought experienced by Bikaner State, court artists painted murals of clouds and rainfall to share this phenomenon with royal children who had never seen it.

Right across Rajasthan, from south-west to north-east, the Aravalli range, 'Refuge of Strength', forms a rocky spine over 1,500 metres above the surrounding plain, rising at sacred Mount Abu in the south. In the west, this range straddles the low, sandy region of Marwar, 'The Land of the Dead'; the fortified citadels of Jodhpur and Jaisalmer stand on a short branch of the range dividing Marwar from the hillier, fertile district of Mewar in the east, where the rulers of its last capital, Udaipur, were the acknowledged heads of the thirty-six royal houses of Rajasthan. A final spine of the Aravallis ends in The Ridge in Old Delhi, scene of some of the bloodiest battles of the 1857–58 conflict between the British and the rebellious Indian troops.

Some five thousand years ago, early civilized peoples belonging to the Harappan or Indus Valley cultures of what is now Pakistan established urban settlements in northern Rajasthan, while in various districts, from Ahar near Udaipur in the south to the extreme north in Bikaner, ancient copper mines dating from the third millennium BC have been discovered. Round about 2000 BC several Aryan tribes reached the Indian subcontinent, conquering the Harappans, spreading their influence and bringing with them the Sanskrit language, ideas which developed into the caste system, and a religion that absorbed many of the beliefs and deities of the earlier Dravidian population.

From the excavations at Ahar we find traces of Iranian influence in the pottery of three and four thousand years ago. Indeed, the Punjab, on present-day Rajasthan's northern borders, was once a Persian satrapy; and in the second century BC it was one of Alexander the Great's provinces, ruled by a pure Greek, Menander, who waged war in Rajasthan.

Buddhism left its mark here too. Halfway between Jaipur and Alwar, near the village of Bairat, are the remains of the oldest known freestanding structure in all India. A great circular wall encloses the smaller circle of a Buddhist chaitya or chapel; nearby is a monastery dating from the third century BC when Ashoka left one of his famous edicts carved on a rock.

Later came more invaders from the north and the steppes of Central Asia: nomadic tribes such as the Parthians, Scythians (or Sakas), Kushans, White Huns, Gujars and Mongols.

With the coming of the Mongols from Central Asia by way of Afghanistan in the eleventh and twelfth centuries, many exotic Hindu sculptures were mutilated and temples destroyed or converted into mosques. Rajasthan's warrior princes were engaged in battles to the death in order to defend their territory and the honour of their lovely women, and the spasmodic struggles for power continued until the British came on the scene in the eighteenth and nineteenth centuries.

The scorched brick and broken, carved stones of great fortified cities such as Chitor and Ranthambhor testify to countless fights against overwhelming odds – battles for power, for the avenging of some slight on the honour of a lady, battles doomed to defeat, which the defenders transformed into undying glory. Men and women bedecked in bridal robes performed the final sacrifice of *jauhar*, fighting to the death, or like the lovely

5 A general view over the city of Jodhpur from the fifteenth-century fort

Overleaf

6 A floating pavilion on the lake at Alwar

7 A water-distributor at her stall in Udaipur

8 A woman fetching the evening water-supply, near Kharda lake. Her arms are covered in ivory bangles

9 Pilgrims signal the dawn *puja* with offerings to birds and fish at the sacred Pushkar lake

queen Padmini, with fourteen thousand royal ladies, throwing themselves into a furnace rather than facing the shame of capture.

Throughout Rajasthan are mementoes of fiery suicides. At the entrance to palaces and fortresses are the red-painted impressions of delicate palms, mute testimony to the queens who chose self-immolation on their husbands' funeral pyres, thus hoping to join their beloveds swiftly in the hereafter.

As reminders of happier times one can indulge in the splendour of royal palaces, once the private residences of princes but now transformed into hotels, some still staffed by ageing retainers of the former rulers. Amid this magnificence the nomadic tribal Bhils, descendants of some of the earliest inhabitants of this land and themselves erstwhile chieftains of Rajasthan, still live a humble, poverty-stricken existence. Yet their distinguished past has not been forgotten. The Rajput princes of Mewar, offspring of the Sun, could not ascend the *gadi* or throne of Udaipur without their Bhil subjects playing a vital role in the inauguration ceremonies.

Is it paradoxical that this desert land of ferocious summer heat is also a blaze of incredible colour? The colour is the work of man rather than nature. The Rajputs have countered the parched landscape with vibrant rainbow hues in their gay, everyday costumes and in the naïvely charming folk-art murals on their houses which celebrate a family wedding with prancing horses bearing sword-wielding nobles, beauteous maidens, caparisoned elephants and blue-faced gods.

Even the poorest village street is decorated in vivid colour. The women are clad like princesses in full, swinging *ghaghara* skirts with thirty-six metres of scarlet, shocking pink, blazing yellow, purple or emerald material. To complete the costume, they wear tight, backless bodices called *kancholis* and drape *odhnis*, transparent veils sparkling with glitter, over their dark locks. The men, too, stride like princes, twirling luxuriant black moustaches given a warrior's upward twist, their turbans of brilliant orange or scarlet worn like crowns. Perhaps most impressive are the old men with their full white beards parted in the middle and brushed outward and upward to meet the curling ends of their moustaches. Not for nothing are these called Rajputs, 'Sons of Kings'.

Religion plays a vital and usually joyous part in every Rajput's life, not only at festival time. The humblest shrine is treated with reverence. It may be no more than an animistic symbol, a smooth stone, coloured brilliant red or covered with silver leaf and garlands of marigolds and jasmine; a venerable tree, usually a banyan with its aerial roots forming slender columns, or a wild fig tree, the peepul, so often depicted on prehistoric pottery. These too are splashed with the sacred vermilion colour, silent testimony to one of the oldest forms of worship, which will still preserve a sacred tree even if it hampers traffic on a busy city road.

10 A school in the Shiva temple at Mahamandir, on the outskirts of Jodhpur

Overleaf

11 Women washing their utensils at Amar Singh's cenotaph, Nagaur

12 A camel, Sikar. Saris are drying in the background

In this predominantly Hindu land, important Muslim festivals are celebrated with equal enthusiasm. The Urs of Khwaja Muinuddin Chishti at Ajmer attracts thousands of devout Muslims from all over India as well as from neighbouring Muslim countries, Pakistan, Afghanistan and Iran, for this is one of the holiest Muslim sanctuaries in the subcontinent, and is also attended by large numbers of Sikhs and Hindus.

The wayside temples and picturesque shrines usually welcome passing strangers, even non-Hindus, to their holy places. Families taking a break from working in the fields may offer to share their simple midday meal. And in the complex ruins of ancient cities, small boys proudly show off their English, glorying in their past history and eager to share it with the stranger.

But not all fortified cities are deserted. Jaisalmer, built of honey-coloured limestone, is a fairytale capital in the north-western desert, set like a precious jewel in the protective seas of sand. Yet once you pass through its massive, narrow entrance and up the strategically dog-legged approach, you find yourself in the narrow lanes of a living medieval city, embellished with ornately decorated *havelis* or mansions, busy market-places, active temples where once the ancient Asva Puja horse worship was held, and an inner twelfth-century citadel with its fort and palaces. Marco Polo, the adventurous thirteenth-century Italian merchant, visited the old city when it was still an important stage on the fabled Silk Road to China. Some five hundred families still live inside the fortified city today, and of all the ancient capitals of the province it is one of the most enchanting.

Rajasthan is all this and more. It is arid deserts baking under a bronze sky, forests of towering trees amid perfumed flower-gardens on the cool heights of Mount Abu with its famed, elaborately carved marble temples. It is fairy palaces floating on tranquil lakes, and wild life sanctuaries, once the private game reserves of princes, but now sheltering threatened animal and bird species. It is deep gorges with rushing rivers and thickly wooded forests in whose deep shade prowl tigers, panthers and wild boar. It is the furnace-like quarries where men and women still work the fine white marble used to fashion such exquisite monuments as the Taj Mahal, and where the skilful stone masons of Makrana still cut and shape the marble with the delicate craftsmanship of their ancestors. It is the freshness of an early morning with graceful village women swinging their skirts as they carry brass water-pots on their proudly held heads.

There have been many changes in the past few decades – independence for India, the partition that divided Hindu and Muslim, the changing of the name from Rajputana to its original Rajasthan and the introduction of the law that deprived the princes of their titles and privileges – yet Rajasthan has not lost its unique qualities.

If anything can conjure up the excitement and colour of this enchanting region it is Roloff Beny's photographs. He brings to it the vision of an artist who observes and immortalizes unusual aspects of everyday life.

Let us hope that between us we may stimulate the imagination of the reader who has never been to India, and refresh the memories of those who know and love this glorious and romantic land.

SYLVIA A. MATHESON

13 Crowds on their way to a *mela*

I
THE
PROUD & ANGRY
DUST

The Aryan, the non-Aryan,
the Dravidian,
The Huns, the Pathans and the Moghuls —
They have all merged here into one body.

Rabindranath Tagore, *A Flight of Swans*

The troubles of our proud and angry dust
are from eternity and shall not fail . . .

A. E. Housman, Introduction to *Last Poems*

CHAPTER ONE
The Land and its History

A harsh land, carved out of burning deserts and mountains, forested valleys and hills and peopled by descendants of the sun and the moon. This land has a turbulent history, with that terrifying code of chivalry which we glimpsed in the prologue. Here the heat of summer becomes intolerable, killing plant and animal life. The blessed advent of the torrential monsoon rains in June brings relief to the parched, thirsty earth and dehydrated peoples – that is, unless the monsoon fails or, equally disastrous, devastates with widespread floods.

Yet this is also a country of surprisingly gentle beauty and a history dating from the earliest known civilizations of the subcontinent. Even then, it was no jungle of primitive savages. Kalibangan, a prehistoric site in northern Bikaner, was an important walled city inhabited even earlier than Harappa, and many third-millennium copper-smelting centres have been found in Rajasthan by the noted Indian archaeologist, Dr R. C. Agrawal.

Most authorities believe the original inhabitants of Rajasthan came from what is now Baluchistan, to the west of the River Indus, or possibly from Iran, further west still; they brought influences from the Sumerians living by the Tigris and Euphrates. Whoever they were, the peoples of the Indus Valley cultures built well-designed cities to a uniform plan, with main streets nearly ten metres wide and splendid public and domestic buildings often several storeys high, constructed around square courtyards, with bathrooms and drains flowing into sewers covered by brick slabs and running to soakpits – far better living conditions than in many towns on the subcontinent today.

Particularly interesting is the link between the primitive religion of these peoples, and present-day Hinduism as practised in Rajasthan. For instance, the Harappa seals include one showing a nude god with a horned headdress, surrounded by wild animals, elephant, rhinoceros, buffalo and tiger, and two deer below his stool. Plant life grows from the god's head and there are possibly two other faces on the image. From the connection with Lord Shiva, widely worshipped today and sometimes depicted with three faces, and also known as 'The Lord of Beasts', a fertility deity, the ancient Indus Valley god has been called 'proto-Shiva'.

Certain trees such as the peepul, widely revered today, were sacred five thousand years ago; phallic worship was also important, then as now, when present-day Shiva temples display the *lingam* or phallic symbol.

From skeletal remains we learn that the ancient peoples of Harappa (called Dasyus and Panis in the collection of religious verses known as the Vedas), were long-headed, narrow-nosed and slender, a Mediterranean type found all over the ancient Middle East and Egypt. There was another

14 Camels, indispensable in this desert land, are highly prized for transport and in Bikaner's noted Camel Corps

element here too, the Proto-Australoid; these were Dasa (literally 'slave' or 'bondsman'), with flat noses and thick lips, characteristics which are seen in some of the older Rajasthan hill tribes.

Such were the men and women whose cities were established in Rajasthan, only to be conquered and left deserted by successive waves of Aryan invaders. The first bands of horse-riding nomads destroyed villages in Baluchistan, driving refugees to seek the protection of the larger, walled cities. And by the middle of the second millennium BC, the invaders reached the cities themselves, most of whose inhabitants had sufficient warning to flee, taking their valuables with them.

The newcomers were tall, comparatively fair-skinned and equipped with light war-chariots with spoked wheels drawn by pairs of horses, a great improvement on the lumbering, solid-wheeled ass- or ox-drawn carts of the Indus Valley peoples. The Aryans also had much superior weapons. With these advantages they conquered not only north-western India, but Europe as well, becoming the ancestors of Greeks, Celts, Latins and the Teutonic races. They called themselves Aryas but their name was transformed into the better-known Aryan – Eire and Iran are versions of the same name.

With them the Aryans brought a new language, Sanskrit, which became the basis of all the present-day Indo-European languages; they also brought their sky gods, Indra, god of war and of weather; Surya or Vishnu, the sun god; Agni, the god of fire, and many others, absorbed into later Hinduism. Half-submerged in the Naval Sagar Lake in the Rajput State of Bundi is still a temple to Varuna, the Aryan god of wind, while many sun temples are scattered throughout the country.

Aryan priests composed hymns in praise of these gods, to be sung at sacrificial ceremonies such as the Asvamedha or horse sacrifice which was to have a special influence on later Rajasthan. The hymns, known collectively as the Rig Veda, were originally handed down by word of mouth and preserved through brilliant feats of memory, to survive today recited by devout Brahmins. The prayers, many based on historical fact, tell us that the Aryans were pantheistic, believing that God is everything and everything is God; they readily absorbed local deities of the conquered peoples, and thus over the centuries there evolved the elaborate ritual of present-day Hinduism, described in greater detail in another chapter.

The Aryans eventually divided their society into four major sects known collectively as 'Varna', literally 'coloured', suggesting the development of the old tribal class structure based on conquered peoples of differing complexions and cultures. First came the priests, the Brahmins, then the warriors, Kshatriyas; thirdly, farmers and traders, who were Vaisyas, and lastly the menial workers and labourers, including the conquered Dravidians – these were the Sudras. The four divisions were fairly flexible in the beginning but later evolved into the rigid classes known today, when an orthodox Hindu born into one caste can never hope to change his status or marry into another.

The great battle of Kurukshetra, involving the whole of India, probably took place about the beginning of the ninth century BC near modern Delhi, and was immortalized in the world's longest poem, the Mahabharata, first written down about the fourth century BC and subsequently added to over a

15 The rippling sands of the desert around Bikaner

period of centuries. The Mahabharata is about seven times as long as the Iliad and the Odyssey combined and its setting is mainly in or around Rajasthan. It includes a sermon known as the Bhagavad Gita – 'The Song of God' – expounded by Krishna, Chief of the Yadava tribe and the seventh incarnation of Lord Vishnu; philosophy, theology and many dramatic and romantic legends, including the story of the five Pandava brothers, are all in the Gita.

The epic of the Pandavas tells how the Princess Draupati chose one of them, the warrior prince Arjun, as her bridegroom in a peculiarly Rajput ceremony known as the *Swayamvara*. Deprived of their rightful heritage, the brothers were exiled for thirteen years which they spent wandering in the forests of Rajasthan. Princess Draupati shared their exile as wife of all five – when Arjun and his brothers rushed to their mother to announce they had brought home a great treasure, their mother, unaware of the identity of the 'treasure', had ordered them to share it equally, hence the joint wife.

Their exile over, the brothers, helped by Krishna, successfully fought their unscrupulous cousins the Kauravas, in a battle north of Delhi. But it was an empty victory, for all the most important Indian kings had been killed and only the Pandavas and Krishna survived.

The other great Indian epic is the Ramayana, a mixture of history, legend, folklore and philosophy, some of which is incorporated in the later Mahabharata. The Ramayana is believed to have originated in oral form about 1500 BC and was written in verse form by a sage called Valmiki, about the fifth century BC. It describes how Aryan chieftains battled for supremacy in India and is another tale of royal intrigue, a dispossessed prince, Rama (the earthly incarnation of the god Vishnu) and his faithful wife Sita whose hand he won in an archery contest. Sita's abduction by the demon King Ravan of Lanka (Sri Lanka), and her rescue with the help of the monkey god, Hanuman, is the subject of many paintings and sculptures in temples and palaces all over Rajasthan. During the ten-day festival of Diwali the dramatic story is enacted by itinerant players throughout the country.

Any visitor to India should know something of the background of these two epics, given here in only the briefest outline. Even recognizing the identities of Sita and Rama, Hanuman, Lord Krishna and the many others depicted in folk art will add to the enjoyment of travelling, especially through the towns and villages of Rajasthan, such as Chandravati near Jhalrapatan, where so much of the Pandava story is said to have taken place.

By the time Buddha came on the scene in the sixth century BC, the Aryans had penetrated the lower reaches of the Chambal River, which runs through southern Rajasthan, and had settled in Malwa, the territory being now divided into small kingdoms with permanent capitals. The Mahabharata recognized a number of republican tribes in Rajasthan, one of the most important being the Yaudheyas, whose coins with inscriptions, titles and official seals have been found with other third-century BC inscriptions referring to the Malava tribe, probably the founders of a dating system known as 'the Era of Vikrama'. They may have been the tribe described by Greek historians as Malloi, living in the Punjab at the time of Alexander's invasion. Alexander reached the Indus Valley and after great difficulties defeated an Indian king, Porus, probably ruler of the old Kuru tribe,

*Whatever man gives me
In true devotion;
Fruit or water,
A leaf, a flower;
I will accept it.
That gift is love,
His heart's dedication.*
                    Bhagavad Gita

16 One of the many inscriptions carved by the Emperor Ashoka in the third century BC can be seen on this rock near Bairat

Overleaf

17 People washing their clothes and their children in the Chambal river at Kota

successors to the Bharatas of northern Rajasthan. The king was described as being a handsome man, tall and courageous. When he was brought before Alexander he was suffering from no less than nine wounds, but when asked how he wished to be treated, he replied proudly, 'As befits me, like a king.' Alexander was so impressed that he gave him back his kingdom to rule as a vassal, and left him in charge of the Punjab.

We have no evidence that Alexander himself ever reached Rajasthan, but Greek influence is to be seen in temple buildings and sculptures, while coins of Alexander the Great were found at Bairat, a small town between Jaipur and Alwar.

Round about the year 305 BC, soon after Alexander reached India, Chandragupta Maurya rose to power in the area and met Seleucus Nicator, Alexander's satrap, in battle. In fact he gained part of Afghanistan as a result of his victory and may have given one of his daughters in marriage to Seleucus whose ambassador, Megasthenes, left a vivid description of the splendid Mauryan palaces and rich court life. The Mauryan dynasty adopted the peacock as their heraldic symbol, a bird sacred largely because of its colour, the same as Lord Krishna's countenance, always depicted as dark blue.

The peacock is the sacred vehicle of Saraswati, goddess of learning and the arts and wife of Brahma the Creator, and also of Lord Shiva's second son, Karttikeya god of war, and is found wild all over Rajasthan. Rudyard Kipling's father Lockwood Kipling, in his delightful book *Beast and Man in India* quotes a proverb which says, 'The deer, the monkey, the partridge and the peacock are four thieves', but they are never punished.

When they scent the coming of the rains, peacocks scream and dance with delight. Sometimes, wrote Kipling, peacocks are caught alive by villagers and taken to market with their eyelids sewn up with filaments of their own quills, to stop them fluttering and spoiling their plumage.

Ashoka, Chandragupta's grandson, a great humanist, administrator and provider for his people, ordered wells dug and rest-houses built for travellers; to commemorate these deeds he left the oldest surviving Indian inscriptions on rocks and pillars throughout his empire, including one at Bairat, where the Pandava heroes of the Mahabharata took refuge. The inscription proves that Rajasthan was in Ashoka's empire and would seem to indicate that it was here the emperor entered the monastic order in the Buddhist *vihara* whose stone ruins crown the hill above.

The Mauryans were followed by waves of fresh invaders: Bactrian Greeks from northern Afghanistan, the Chinese Yueh-Chih from Central Asia who were known as Kushans in India, and the Sakas or Scythians, also from Bactria – superb horsemen these, from whom many Rajputs believe they are descended. Most of the medieval Rajput clans are believed to come from a mixture of earlier, indigenous hill tribes and settled Hun invaders of the fifth century, who destroyed or dispersed the ancient martial Rajput.

Scythians of differing clans and dynasties remained in India for something like six hundred years and evidence of their presence in Rajasthan is given in a second-century AD inscription carved on a stone by a Scythian ruler of Kutch, a coastal region south-west of Rajasthan. Famed as metal-workers, they no doubt brought their craft to this new region, laying the foundations of the art of metal-casting which has produced some outstanding works of bronze from Rajasthan.

Many people believe that the gypsies found all over Europe today are the offspring of Scythian and indigenous Rajput marriages, and there are elements of similarity in their traditions, customs and language.

During the Scythian period the Kushans, speaking an Iranian language, arrived in India. Their most famous ruler, Kanishka, a great advocate of Buddhism and a patron of Gandhara art, ruled all the western half of Northern India during the first century AD, establishing settlements in Rajasthan too. Eventually the Scythians were defeated by a new Chandra Gupta, grandson of the founder of the Guptas, who, soon after 388 AD, became paramount ruler of almost all northern India, including Rajasthan. He is responsible for establishing the 'prosperous and happy empire' mentioned by the Chinese traveller Fa-Hsien, who wrote that it was possible to travel from one end of the country to the other without molestation or need of passports; as A. L. Basham has observed in *The Wonder that was India*, the region at this time was probably the happiest and most civilized in the world.

Gupta art, particularly sculpture and architecture, marked a high peak of cultural achievement in ancient India, while one of the most famous Sanskrit poets and playwrights, Kalidasa, made Kansua, near Kota, the setting for his play *Shakuntala*. Gupta temples are found at Mandor (the royal gardens of Jodhpur), and in the forests around the ancient city of Jhalrapatan, in Jhalawar.

It was during this Gupta period that yet more Central Asian invaders appeared on the scene; these were the Hephthalites or White Huns, a Turko-Mongol people who, during the fifth century AD, broke the power of the Guptas and ruled Western India including Rajasthan for some thirty years, during which they practically wiped out Buddhism. Meanwhile a descendant of the second Gupta line, sixteen-year-old Harsha, ascended the throne in 606 AD, reviving the dynasty whose descendants were to rise to power centuries later as the Rathores of Marwar, and whose rulers towards the end of the seventh century were among the last great Indian monarchs to perform the Vedic horse sacrifice ceremony. Harsha himself ruled an extensive empire from his capital of Kanauj near modern Kanpur, where he established many Buddhist and Hindu temples.

During the ninth and tenth centuries another clan which probably originated in Rajasthan, the Gurjara-Pratiharas, rose to power, successfully resisting the Arabs who had brought the new religion of Islam to the western part of the country. Then came the fierce Ghaznavids, Sabuktagin and his son, Mahmud of Ghazni, pouring out of Afghanistan to make no less than seventeen devastating raids into India; palaces and temples were looted and destroyed and vast numbers of people enslaved. Many petty chieftains succumbed to the Ghaznavids but the Chauhan dynasty of Rajasthan successfully resisted them, and themselves rose to power in the area. However, they were surrounded by many other independent Hindu rulers and by the end of the twelfth century the three chief monarchs of Northern India, Prithviraj Chauhan, Jaichand Gaharwar and Parmal Chandel, were warring among themselves until they were confronted with yet more

Afghan invaders led by Muhammad Ghori. In 1192, Ghori defeated and killed Prithviraj III of Ajmer, who was leading the defence of Delhi, together with some 150 Rajput princes and their armies, and Prithviraj's stout resistance and romantic love story are cited today as the epitome of Rajput chivalry and courage.

His is a typical Montague and Capulet romance. The prince's family had long been at loggerheads with the Kanauj rulers, Harsha's descendants, but the Kanauj princess, Sanyukta, had fallen in love with Prithviraj. At that time princesses of great houses had a certain amount of freedom in choosing their bridegrooms in the ceremony called *Swayamvara*: select suitors were invited to the court and the princess would indicate her choice by garlanding one of the gathering. In this instance Sanyukta's father refused to invite Prithviraj and had erected his statue in a humiliating position as doorkeeper by one of the side entrances to the fort. Defying her father, the princess ignored the other eligible princes and draped her garland round the statue. Thus encouraged, Prithviraj made a daring raid into the Kanauj stronghold and carried off his bride, thereby naturally intensifying the feud between the two families. When Prithviraj met his death in the battle for Delhi, his bride chose to mount her husband's funeral pyre and perish with his corpse.

Prithviraj's death weakened the Chauhan clan, scattering many of them far from their homeland. Some found sanctuary in the Rajput state of Mewar with its famous fortress city of Chitor. And the descendants of Princess Sanyukta's family, fleeing from the victorious Ghoris who now ruled Delhi and Kanauj, took refuge in Gujarat, south of Rajasthan. Later these appeared as the Rathore clan of Marwar, taking with them the symbol of the Kanauj monarchy, a seventh-century sandalwood *gadi* or throne known as the 'Pugal'.

About 1500 AD, in a break from the Jodhpur house, a younger son of the family established his own state of Bikaner, taking his heritage of the 'Pugal', which is probably the oldest piece of furniture surviving in India today. Look for it when you visit the Junagadh palace in Bikaner. You may be able to persuade the guardian to lift the covers and reveal wheels, stars and flowers carved in a style reminiscent of the ninth-century Abbasid palace of Samarra.

From now on Rajput history is that of the increasingly powerful princes claiming legendary descent from the sun, moon and fire, but all belonging to the Kshatriya or warrior caste. Time and time again Rajput strongholds such as Chitor, Ranthambhor, Jodhpur and many others were attacked by Muslim armies: Alauddin Khilji in the early fourteenth century; the Emperor Babur, Bahadur Shah of Gujarat and Emperor Akbar in the sixteenth century. In fact, after five hundred years of Muslim rule in India, Rajasthan was the only part of the country, excepting the southernmost tip, still almost entirely Hindu. When the Mughals finally demonstrated that they were the effective rulers, most Rajput princes accepted the fact, many diplomatically giving their daughters as wives to the emperors and themselves rising high in the military and administrative service of the

18 Sunrise: women carrying water up the ghats by the lake at Pushkar

Colonel Tod presents his credentials to the Maharana Bhim Singh, fresco in Udaipur City Palace

empire. From the time of Akbar, Mughal emperors had made it a policy to consolidate their conquests by taking Rajput princesses into their harems, often as principal queens. The first of several of Akbar's Rajput wives was the daughter of the ruler of Amber (soon to become Jaipur State), in 1562, and she became the mother of the next emperor, Jahangir, who in turn married the Amber ruler's sister. Shah Jahan and Aurangzeb were also sons of Rajput princesses and Akbar himself was often seen wearing typical Rajput costume.

With the gradual decline of the Mughal empire came British influence in the form of the East India Company. The British were no strangers to Rajasthan. In Ajmer, for instance, strategically held by many different rulers throughout its turbulent history, Sir Thomas Roe, England's first official ambassador to India, sent by King James I to the court of the Emperor Jahangir, arrived in 1616 to present his credentials. While living in Ajmer he took the opportunity of touring other parts of Rajasthan, including the dramatically ruined fortress of Chitor, which only fifty years earlier had been sacked by Akbar for the third and last time, and Sir Thomas left a fascinating account of daily life in the Emperor's magnificent 'camp'.

Through intermarriage and cooperation with the Mughal emperors, the Rajput princes still maintained a certain amount of independence. When the British finally came to power in India, British Political Agents were sent as advisers to many of the states, the Chief Commissioner administering the region from Ajmer. Most of the Political Officers became strongly attached to their princes and did much to settle old rivalries, stabilize the political situation and bring a closer understanding of these historic peoples to the more distant British administrators in the then capital of Calcutta.

One of the most outstanding administrators was Colonel James Tod, author of the *Annals and Antiquities of Rajasthan* (indispensable for any serious student of the area). Born in England in 1782 and dying there in 1835, he first visited India in 1798 when he obtained a cadetship in the East India Company. His introduction to Rajasthan came with a visit from neighbouring Gwalior State to Mewar in 1806. Tod immediately fell in love with the country and began his research into the traditions and history of Rajasthan, staying in the area until 1822. For the last four years he was Political Agent, preparing maps of the States, much of which had been a geographical blank until that time. Speaking Persian, Urdu, Arabic, Hindi and many local dialects including Rajasthani, he gained the love and respect of the Rajputs, and to quote his own feelings, 'If we compare the antiquity and illustrious descent of dynasties which have ruled the small sovereignties of Rajasthan, with many of celebrity in Europe, superiority will often attach to the Rajput...'

James Tod had various theories about the origins of the Rajputs, some of which have been disproved, while others are now receiving a closer investigation by modern researchers. But whether in fact they trace their descent from the Sakas, the Hephthalites or anyone else, the fact remains that Rajput traditions and culture do include many and varied ancient customs and beliefs that have helped mould the distinctive character that so impressed Tod. Rajasthan is unique in all India, and this fascinating land still echoes with the distant sounds of fiery battles and deeds of valour.

19 A wayside shrine at Bairat

CHAPTER TWO

The Romance of the States

Of the four original great states of Rajasthan (Udaipur, formerly Mewar; Jodhpur, originally Marwar; Jaipur, erstwhile Dhundapur, and Bundi) Udaipur is the premier, its ruler acknowledged as foremost among the Rajput princes. The Guhilot dynasty of Mewar is the only one to have ruled the same territory for twelve centuries despite numerous invasions, and they are the only Hindu princes to refuse the political advantages of intermarrying with Mughal emperors. Mewar was originally about the size of present-day Switzerland, and its first capital was Dhulkot, where archaeological excavations are now taking place on the ancient site of Tambawati Nagri near the village of Ahar. Later the capital was moved to the spectacular clifftop of Chitor where it remained until, in the sixteenth century, the ruler created a new capital, Udaipur.

Claiming descent from Surya the Sun God, through Rama, the royal family originated about the first century AD near the Kashmir border, moving south in the second century to annex the territory of a Paramara prince. One of the fourth-century rulers of Mewar, King Chandravarman of Pushkarana, was immortalized in a Sanskrit inscription recording his heroic deeds, on the famous Iron Pillar in Delhi's Qutb Minar.

About 525 AD their city of Valabhi on the western (Gujarat) coast of India was sacked by invaders and the entire royal family wiped out with the exception of the chief queen, Pushpavati. Heavily pregnant, she was on a pilgrimage to the sacred shrine of Amba-Bhavani where she offered a sacrifice for the coming baby. When the news of her husband's death was brought, she found sanctuary with a family of Brahmin priests in a cave in the Aravalli Hills. Here she gave birth to a son who was named Goha or Guhil (cave-born) and who was to found the Guhilot dynasty, later known as the Sisodias after a small town of that name.

Once Queen Pushpavati was sure of the succession she had her own funeral pyre constructed and threw herself into its flames. But before committing ritual suicide she entrusted the baby prince to the daughter of a temple priest.

By the time he was eleven, the prince was spending most of his time in the forest with the Bhils, a hill tribe believed to be descendants of the late Stone Age hunters whose land this was originally. Guhil was a born leader and one anecdote often recounted by bardic singers tells how the Bhil children were playing when the chieftain's son accidentally cut his thumb. Immediately he pressed it against Guhil's forehead, giving him the *tika* of sovereignty, a title later confirmed by the chieftain himself, Mandalika, who gave Guhil his first territory, a stretch of forested mountain. Right up until the abolition of the princes, Bhil chieftains played this essential role in the

20 The pavilions of Shah Jahan on Anasagar lake, Ajmer. This view is from the Circuit House, formerly the British Residency and now a hotel

investiture of the Mewar rulers, drawing blood from a cut on their own thumbs. After marking the new Rana's forehead, the Bhil chieftain would take the prince by the arm and seat him on the throne. A second important Bhil chieftain would hold a salver of spices and sacred grains of rice.

For eight generations the Guhilots lived in the same area until about 734 AD, when the eighth prince was killed by Bhils while hunting. A descendant of the Brahmin woman who had saved young Guhil rescued the three-year-old heir, Bappa Rawal, taking the child first to a fortress in a remote area of neighbouring Gwalior, then to Nagda between Ranakpur and Udaipur.

Here, in the hidden valleys, Bappa tended the sacred cows, and many stories are told of the royal cowherd's adventures. Colonel Tod relates one prank that led to another flight for life when Bappa encountered the daughter of the Solanki chieftain of Nagda, accompanied by some six hundred village maidens, who asked the youth to find them ropes for their swings. He agreed on condition that first they played a game of make-believe marriage, with himself as the bridegroom, and Solankini, the chief's daughter, as the bride. Not long afterwards Solankini's parents prepared her wedding to a neighbouring prince, but the priests, reading the girl's palm, discovered she was already married – a great disgrace for the bride's family – and the hunt was on for the culprit. Bappa found refuge with two faithful Bhil companions whose descendants were to take part in future investiture ceremonies.

Legendary founder of the Kachhwahas of Amber/Jaipur, the tenth-century Dhola Rai has a similar history of an upbringing with tribal folk, in this instance, the Minas. The Kachhwahas also claim descent from the Sun through Rama's second son Kusa, whose descendants founded Gwalior. Dhola Rai, infant heir to his father's kingdom, was cheated by his uncle who usurped the throne on the death of his brother. The baby's mother, dressed as a servant, fled carrying the child in a basket. After many adventures the child was adopted by the Mina chieftain, but later repaid his benefactor's generosity by annexing his territory through trickery. Eventually he was ambushed and killed by vengeful tribesmen. However, his grandson conquered the hilltop city of Amber, then capital of another Mina tribe, and founded the Rajput State of Jaipur.

The other important solar family is that of the Rathores, descendants of the powerful Guptas whose country is Marwar, the desert 'Land of the Dead', in contrast to the fertile valleys of Mewar to the east. Colonel Tod believed that the Rathores' ancestors were Scythians. According to their own traditions, a chieftain, Nain Pal, conquered the wealthy north Indian city of Kanauj in 470 AD. The dynasty remained there for the next seven hundred years until, in 1193, Muslims from Ghor in central Afghanistan captured the city. Forced to flee, Jaichand, the last ruler, is said to have drowned in the Ganges, his body being identified only by his false teeth. Eighteen years later his grandson or possibly his son, Siahji, who had managed to retain the ancient Kanauj throne as well as some two hundred followers, arrived in the arid Thar desert to offer his services to the local Solanki prince.

After winning a notable battle for his patron, Siahji was rewarded by marriage to the ruler's sister, together with a generous dowry. After many

21 The Keoladeo Ghana bird sanctuary, near Bharatpur, was originally created as an enormous private shoot. Now it is a refuge for birds, and animals such as this buffalo

more battles and wanderings, including a certain amount of double-dealing, Siahji set himself up as ruler of extensive lands around Pali, a thriving trade centre on important caravan routes, and today a small industrial town between Jodhpur and Ranakpur.

Siahji's descendants were prolific both in their offspring and their conquests and by the late fourteenth century were rulers, under Chanda, of extensive lands including Mandor and Nagaur. Chanda's eldest son, Rainmal, a giant of a man and a famous athlete, captured Ajmer, restoring it to Mewar, and was later invited by his sister to act as Regent for her orphaned son, heir to the fortified hilltop city of Chitorgarh. Through palace intrigues Rainmal was plied with opium and tied to his bed with his own turban, many yards long. Attacked then by his enemies he managed to stand, although still befuddled and attached to his bed, and defended himself with a brass waterpot, but he was shot dead.

Remembering this in later years, Rainmal's grandson, Bika, always slept on a short bed (which can be seen today in Bikaner's Phul Mahal), lest the same fate happen to him, when at least he would be able to stand more easily to defend himself. The bitter feuds that resulted in Rainmal's assassination ended in Mewar and Marwar being divided into two completely separate states.

In 1459, when he was fifteen, Rainmal's eldest son Rao Jodha escaped and regained his capital of Mandor where the Rathores occupied the ancient castles on craggy hills above a fertile gorge. Today Mandor is a magnet for visitors to the lush gardens surrounding royal cenotaphs and magnificent temples, and the famous Hall of Heroes carved into the cliffside.

Legend tells how young prince Jodha, riding alone, was attacked by his enemies near the steep escarpment of a rocky outcrop called the Birds' Nest, escaping by frantically scaling the almost sheer cliff. In doing so he stumbled on the hermitage of a holy man, by a spring in a cleft of the outcrop. The hermit advised the prince to move his somewhat vulnerable fortress at Mandor to the Birds' Nest, and so today you can wander through a vast complex of palaces on the top of this dramatic cliff, reached through seven fortified gateways, built by Jodha and his successors.

Although there was a lake and a deep well within the fort, both had brackish water, for it seems that Jodha's engineers had included the hermit's own cave in their plans for the castle and the enraged holy man cursed them, saying that all their water would be brackish no matter what they did. Certainly potable water had to be brought on foot up the steep, zigzag path from the Gulab Sagar lake at the bottom of the cliff, until a pump was installed in modern times.

To ensure the invulnerability of the new fortress, a primitive sacrificial custom was carried out, with the burial alive of the unfortunate architect, Bambhi Rajra, in the foundations. (Jodha did give the wretched man's family a generous pension in compensation!)

The northernmost desert state of Bikaner was founded by one of Jodha's younger sons, Bika, whom everyone recognized as being far stronger and much more of a natural leader than his older brothers. Before his father died in about 1500 AD, he made Bika swear never to try and take the throne of Jodhpur; in return he was given a small army with which he could establish his own kingdom elsewhere. Some valuable dynastic heirlooms, including the sandalwood 'Pugal' throne, a royal umbrella, a sword and a horse of 'divine origin', were promised him when he left to seek his fortune, for these heirlooms would give Bika the legal right to found a kingdom. When he tried to claim them, however, his brothers refused to part with them. In a surprise attack, Bika took the Jodhpur fortress with his small though courageous army, but, keeping his promise, he left his elder brothers unharmed, taking only his heritage of the ancient throne and other symbols of power. The throne was almost certainly formed from fragments of the seventh-century 'Pugal' brought by Siahji from Kanauj three centuries earlier.

Bika, with his growing band of adventure-seeking young warriors, fought his way towards the arid desert then known as Jangaldesh, a land where even today the camel is supreme (Bikaner's camel-breeding farm is world-famed), and, being on the old Silk Road to Central Asia, a battleground for would-be conquerors. On his way, Bika paused at the shrine of Deshnoke, offering homage to Karni Mata, a miracle-working woman regarded as the incarnation of the goddess Durga; she prophesied victory, blessing Bika who went on to conquer the territory, making it his own state of Bikaner.

Two powerful neighbouring Jat clans offered Bika supreme, uncontested power in return for protection against their enemies; and like the Guhilots and the Bhils, Bika and his heirs were to receive the *tika* of inauguration only from the elders of one of the Jat tribes.

Relics of Bikaner's founder can be seen in the sixteenth-century Junagadh fort, including the 'Pugal' and two large drums given to Bika by Jamboji, a holy man who predicted that the dynasty would rule for 450 years, which would have brought it to 1940. Bika triumphantly passed this news to an uncle but instead of being pleased, he was furious that Jamboji had not foreseen a longer period of power. Determined to get a more satisfactory forecast, the uncle approached the holy man when he was in a deep trance, and tried to rouse him somewhat roughly by thrusting a brazier of burning incense under his nose! He finally succeeded and Jamboji resignedly told him that the dynasty could have another fifty years 'more or less', but that the extra years would be a period of trial and tribulation: an interesting prediction in view of the final abolition of the rule of the princes in 1971.

The House of Bikaner, descendants of the Sun, has a long history of intermarriage with the Bhatti princesses of neighbouring Jaisalmer who claim descent from the Moon. Like the other Rajput princes, the history of the Bhattis was one of struggle to extend their territory or to defend what they already possessed. Their rulers are called Rawal, 'of the Royal House', a title stemming from the ninth-century treachery on the part of a neighbouring chief whose daughter was to marry the young heir, Deoraj. Deoraj's father and eight hundred of his relatives and followers were massacred at the wedding, and Deoraj himself escaped only with the help of a Brahmin yogi who disguised the prince as a fellow Brahmin, adding the final convincing touch by eating from the same dish as the prince when his enemies came looking for him, something no Brahmin holy man would normally contemplate.

Overleaf

22 Stacks of wheat make a frame for a distant camel with two riders

23 A tea-stall under the walls of the Old Fort at Nagaur

Some time later Deoraj repaid his saviour by stealing his tattered jacket containing a flask of magic elixir, a drop of which had fallen onto the prince's dagger and turned it to gold. With such wealth in his hands he built a stronghold called Derawar, and the magnanimous yogi allowed him to keep his booty on condition that he became his disciple and wore the ochre robe of a holy man. With a begging bowl round his neck, the prince visited his relatives' home and found his gourd was miraculously filled with gold and pearls, the *tika* of investiture placed on his forehead and his new title of 'Rawal' proclaimed.

South of Derawar another Rajput clan had their desert capital at Lodurva, a large city with twelve great gates, which Deoraj captured and made his own capital. Towards the end of the twelfth century came the fulfilment of an old prophecy. Jaisal, eldest son of the Bhatti Rawal and therefore the rightful heir, had been passed over in favour of his younger half-brother. With the aid of Shihabuddin, a Muslim invader from Ghor, Afghanistan, Jaisal captured Lodurva, allowing the Afghan troops to plunder the city for three days, as he had previously agreed, and then moved his capital from the ruins to the triple-peaked mountain of Tricute about sixteen kilometres to the south. The old prophecy had also foretold that the new city – Jaisalmer – would be sacked 'two and a half times', which also came to pass.

Jaisalmer today is one of the most romantic and spectacular of all the Rajput fortresses, its honey-gold stone walls and towers glowing in the sun, its great *havelis*, virtually forerunners of condominium blocks, still occupied by some five thousand families.

Of Lodurva there remains only a Jain temple and a small cluster of shelters for pilgrims, standing on the edge of the sand-covered mounds of the once magnificent city.

One can see that most of the stories of the foundation of the states stem from similar origins. But the elite of all the Rajput clans have a slightly different history. They claim to have sprung from the sacred firepit or Agnikunda on the summit of holy Mount Abu, Rajasthan's Olympus. They are the four Agnikula, 'fireborn' races comprising the twenty-four Chauhan clans, the Solankis, the Paramaras and the Deoras. And of these the Hara Chauhans of Bundi and Kota are regarded as supreme. Each of the four races takes its name from a mythical figure summoned by the prayers of Brahmin priests desperate to protect their sacred fire from the attacks of 'demons' determined to render it impure. The 'demons' were most likely to have been Indo-Scythian invaders trying to stamp out the indigenous religion and the power of the priests.

Founder of the Hara Chauhans was Ishtpal, who lost ('hara') his fortress city of Asi to the forces of Mahmud of Ghazni in 1025. It was one of Ishtpal's descendants, Rao Dewa Hara, King of Patar, who founded Bundi after two of his ancestors were killed by the Ghorid invaders in the twelfth and thirteenth centuries. Dates vary, but Tod recounts that Rao Dewa was summoned to the court of the fifteenth-century Lodi emperor, Sikander, who regarded the growing power of the Haras with apprehension, and kept both the chief and his youngest son as hostages for the good behaviour of the clan. Dewa's horse was famous in Rajput chronicles as being of such mettle

24 Two teams of buffaloes alternately drawing water from a deep desert well

Overleaf

25 Crushing rock on the road between Jaipur and Sikar

26 At Sambhar salt lake, the only one in India producing salt, women carry basketfuls to be weighed

that 'she could cross a stream without wetting her hoof'. Knowing that the Lodi emperor coveted a colt produced by this magnificent mare, Dewa brandished his spear below the emperor's balcony and making the famous declaration, 'Farewell! There are three things Your Majesty must never ask of a Rajput – his horse, his mistress and his sword!', seized an unexpected opportunity to escape and galloped to his native hills flanking the river Bandunal. Here Mina tribes were paying tribute under pressure to Rao Ganga, a distantly related Khichi chieftain. The next time Rao Ganga came to claim his tribute he was confronted by Dewa mounted on his charger. The Khichi was riding an equally celebrated horse and after a fierce hand-to-hand encounter, Dewa chased his opponent to the banks of the Chambal, a wide swiftly-flowing river (now harnessed by a powerful hydro-electric scheme in Kota). The Khichi and his horse leapt from the high cliffs into the fast torrent and safely reached the opposite bank.

'Bravo, Rajput,' called Dewa. 'Let me know your name.'

When Ganga Khichi told him, the Hara chieftain called, 'We are brothers and must no longer be enemies. Let the river be our boundary.'

Dewa had already begun building the rambling fortifications of Bundi on the steep slopes of the Bandunal gorge, and established the kingdom of Haraoti. A charming mural in the Chattar Sali of Bundi palace depicts a Kota prince crossing the Chambal on horseback, watched by two princesses from a castle window.

The adjoining state of Kota was held as a fief by younger Bundi princes until about 1580 when the fourteen-year-old Bundi prince, Madho Singh, gallantly fighting on behalf of the Mughal emperor, was awarded permanent possession of the area.

A few Rajasthan states such as Bharatpur and Dholpur were ruled by Jats whom some authorities believe to be, like the Rajputs, offspring of Central Asian invaders. The chieftains were those who became Rajputs, the sons of kings, while the agricultural community became the Jats. Their own traditions claim that their original homeland was Zabulistan to the west of the Indus and that by the fifth century AD they were in power in the Punjab and Rajasthan.

Bharatpur was a fairly recently established state, founded in 1733 by an audaciously courageous Jat called Suraj Mal who defied the Mughal emperor and captured the gates of Agra fort to install them in his own fortress at Deeg. Later on this palace became the pleasure resort of the rulers. Meanwhile Bharatpur's great fort, which was originally defended by two massive mud walls and deep moats, withstood attacks by the Mughals and the British before it was finally taken by Lord Lake in 1805. In addition to the gates of Agra, two more gates, 'magic doors' of bronze and silver, were brought from Delhi by Suraj Mal's successor, Maharaja Jawahar Singh. The northern gate, the Ashtadhati, was coming back to Rajasthan, for it had originally been captured from Chitor by Alauddin Khilji.

We have barely skimmed the surface of Rajasthan's romantic beginnings, but if the appetite has been whetted, the imagination stirred, the resourceful reader can search out more details from the bibliography provided.

27 Sunset over the city lake at Kota

CHAPTER THREE
Costume, Handicrafts & Other Arts

One does not have far to look for Rajasthani handicrafts – the dazzlingly brilliant costumes worn with elaborate jewellery are unmistakably Rajput, wherever they may be.

One of the specialities is the tie-dye technique, variously known as *potala*, *ikat* or *bandhani*, and at least three designs popular today were mentioned in an eighteenth-century Jaipur work, the Buddhi Vilasa: these are the *Pomacha*, a lotus pattern with big rosettes on a plain yellow ground; the *Chunari*, where knots are arranged in floral patterns or to represent birds and animals, and the *Laharia*, diagonal stripes.

Tie-dyed fabrics of the sixth century AD have been found in Central Asia, and perhaps this technique was brought to Rajasthan by the Kushans or the Hephthalites from that area. In Rajasthan the tied sections are dyed in different colours and the remaining, untied material then bleached, resulting in dark-coloured spots on a light background. Among many Rajput communities a tie-dyed sari is an essential garment for the bride. Such unlikely colour schemes as shocking pink and scarlet, brilliant yellow and purple, vivid lime green with sky blue and violet, somehow look absolutely right under the hot Rajput sun.

With a history of almost unending conflicts among rival princes and invaders alike, the Rajput dress, like many customs, owes its style in part to this martial past. For instance, the exceptionally bulky *pugris* or turbans worn by the menfolk, when tightly bound around the head in times of warfare, gave considerable protection from sword-cuts. Jodhpur riding breeches, named for the princely state where the idea originated, were practical garments for horsemen. The tight-fitting *churidar* pyjamas are ceremonial wear, but for comfort and coolness the *dhoti*, probably the oldest form of dress, worn by peasants and princes alike, is still everyday wear.

Illustrated in ancient sculptures and described in early writings, the *dhoti* is a single strip of cloth usually reaching from waist to ankles, with one end brought up between the legs to form loose trousers. Another piece of material, the *chuddar* or *dupatta*, is thrown around the shoulders. Sometimes a *bandia angarkha*, a full-sleeved, tight-fitting tunic fastened with cords, is worn over the torso, while state and ceremonial occasions demand a *kurta*, a collarless shirt of very fine muslin over which is worn a long, form-fitting coat called the *achkan* or *lamba angarkha*, often of elaborate brocades and silks, which the wealthy fasten with buttons of emeralds and rubies. The whole is topped off with a *pugri* or *safa* – a turban with a long tail – and a jewelled ornament. In eighteenth-century Jaipur the *pugri* was essential wear at court,

28 By the cenotaph at Sikar, two women dry a freshly dyed sari

the *panch-rang*, a five-coloured turban, being an especial mark of honour.

Cummerbunds – *kamarbunds* – of exquisite brocades or delicate, woven or handblocked material, three metres long and one and a quarter wide, were wound around the waist, with the decorated ends hanging down in front, and these too were insignia of honour.

Early costumes for women were similar to those of the men. A single length of brilliantly coloured fabric was fastened around the waist with a *kamarbund* of fine material, perhaps studded with precious stones or embroidered with real gold and silver thread. A narrow piece of clinging material was wrapped around the breasts, and a light veil cast around the shoulders. On special occasions the veil was used to cover the hair. And of course there was always plenty of jewellery to enhance the alluring effect. But these graceful, revealing garments had to be abandoned with the coming of raiders bent on plunder and the capture of women. So the more figure-concealing but colourful dress worn today was devised. In the picturesque little state of Bundi, chopped silver foil is added to the weaving of the everyday *odhni* veil that completes the costume; the silver washes out eventually but while the material is new it has a most attractive effect under the intense sunshine.

Certain colours are worn for specific occasions. A deep midnight blue, regarded as the colour of love, with silver and gold embroidery, is the scheme for Diwali when the return from exile of the famous lovers of the Ramayana epic, Rama and Sita, is celebrated. In Jaipur the ruler, his family and the entire court would wear a blue so deep it was almost black.

Shades of lime green with pastel pinks and white are worn for the Teej festival of swings which takes place in the rainy season, when the parched earth turns green once more, and striped *laharia* materials take precedence.

Red has always been an auspicious colour, and brides are invariably dressed in flaming red and gold. Forty days after the birth of a child, the mother takes her baby to a ceremony known as Suraj-puja, in honour of the Sun God, and both wear yellow garments trimmed with red, for these are the colours of the sun.

For the last full moon of the Hindu year girls wear silver and white; the gay Holi spring festival means red, orange and white costumes, all soon covered with pink and red dye sprayed from syringes or flung in handfuls, while the Gangaur festival following Holi calls for sunshine colours.

JEWELLERY

Everyday wear includes heavy gold *jhumkas* or earrings with bell-shaped ornaments; silver or gold necklaces, called *kantha* or *hasli*, are worn with heavy anklets and bracelets. Newly-married women cover their arms from wrist to elbow with carved ivory or bone bracelets, sometimes dyed red.

Rajasthan (and Jaipur in particular) is noted especially for its classic enamelled jewellery, a heritage from earliest times, for even in the third century before Christ enamelled jewellery was being made at Taxila in the north of India. This art was brought to a peak in the seventeenth and eighteenth centuries, the Mughal period; only the purest gold is used as the basis for the jewellery or ornaments and today's craftsmen are every bit as skilled as their forebears.

29 On the prehistoric mound of Ahar, saris are laid out to dry after being dyed red. In the background are the cenotaphs of the ranas of Udaipur

Overleaf

30 A typical Rajput from Nagaur, with his tie-dyed turban and magnificent beard

31 A salt-worker at the Sambhar works

32 At Kota, in the gorge of the Chambal, a man wearing an immense turban, reminiscent of the period when such turbans would be protection in warfare

The jewellery is encrusted with stones; the *nau ratan*, nine precious or semi-precious stones, is the most popular type. The stones are embedded in the gold, arranged in abstract patterns, or flowers, animals and birds. The reverse side is covered with equally exquisite enamelwork, the colours often produced by grinding precious stones for a longer-lasting effect. This type of art was made popular in Amber, the old capital of Jaipur, by Akbar the Great's Rajput general, Maharaja Man Singh, whose own craftsmen soon developed an individual style, producing almost three-dimensional effects.

MINOR ARTS

Some charming pottery is produced in various parts of Rajasthan, including paper-thin *kagaz* pottery from Alwar, and Bikaner's gold-lacquered pottery. Hand-painted pieces with a floral motif of pale blue, pink and white are popular in Kota and Sanganer near Jaipur, where the whole town is given over to some type of cottage industry. You will find the main square of Sanganer a hive of activity with the washing and dyeing of handmade rag paper. In almost every home small children help their parents soak and stretch the paper on racks, while piles of strawberry pink and mustard yellow dyes wait in readiness by the front door. In small workshops open to the streets, elderly craftsmen paint designs on handmade notepaper, and, more prosaically, in other courtyards women shape stiff paper cones for loudspeakers. Elsewhere in the town, open sheds house long tables where men and women are busily block-printing the renowned Rajput fabrics.

Makrana, another small town near Jaipur, is perpetually enveloped in a cloud of fine white marble dust, for the celebrated quarries that provided the marble for the Taj Mahal are in the midst of the town and are still being worked. Bullock-carts draw heavy blocks of marble through the narrow lanes to be shaped, mainly by hand, in the many small workshops. All produce delicate marble objects, often inlaid with coloured mosaics similar to those still visible in the walls of the Taj Mahal itself.

Lacquerwork is another typically Rajput craft, particularly bracelets from Jaipur and Jodhpur, and toys and furniture from Udaipur.

Then there is the brasswork, intricately engraved and adorned with coloured enamels to form trays, boxes, goblets and such-like. Jaipur is again a centre for some of the finest examples of this craft. Simple, fine engraving is known as *chiken Jaipani*, while the *thalai*, which today is becoming more rare, involves hammering out the design from the back of the article, and a dish made in this style may take four months or more of incessant hard work.

Children's toys are another delightful example of folk art. Puppets and stuffed toys with painted or embroidered features, small clay carts and miniature fruits of clay, and models of Lord Krishna in the shape of a drinking cup in which the water only reaches the deity's feet before draining away, are among the many charming playthings.

Mojaries or soft leather slippers with curly toes and buffalo-hide soles, the uppers embroidered with heavy gold and scarlet thread, are specialities of Jodhpur and Jaipur; camel-skin is a favourite material in the desert states of Jodhpur, Jaisalmer and Bikaner, where articles from water-bottles to chests, slippers, small ornaments and lamps are fashioned from it. Camelhair rugs and blankets woven in stripes and checks are also produced in Jaisalmer.

33 Fresco of a lady in Bundi City Palace

FOLK ART

Phad paintings, which are in scroll form, are peculiarly Rajput and made in Bhilwara, depicting legendary exploits of past heroes. The artist prepares his own canvas, using a paste of wheat starch spread on cloth. He uses five flat colours in strict order: bright red, green, blue, brown and black, and paints his figures in a bold, unsophisticated style. Originally these scrolls could be six metres long and one wide, and even today they can contain up to two hundred panels illustrating a folk story. They are said to have originated with the charts drawn up for horoscopes, with symbols such as a fish, representing the natural waters of a river, a bird, an artificial lake and so on, showing the venue of the story. One popular subject is the history of Pabuji and Phulmati, a pair of star-crossed lovers, and their adventures.

Phad paintings are used as stage backdrops for performances by the Bhopas, wandering minstrels who act out the tales depicted on them.

Another type of painting on cloth is the *pichwai*, a pigment painting whose themes are dedicated to Lord Krishna, depicting episodes from his life. These paintings are hung in the inner sanctuary of Krishna temples, each with a separate theme, and changed to match seasons and ceremonies. One of the best-loved themes is produced in Nathdwara, where the most famous and holiest of all Krishna shrines is situated. It is a reproduction of the shrine's ancient stylized black marble image of Krishna in his form of Srinathji.

Jasleen Dhamija in her book on folk art tells us that the craft of making *pichwais* originated in Mathura and Brindaban, the area where Krishna is said to have been born. Rough, handspun cloth is used as the basic canvas for *pichwais*, after a thin layer of starch and pigment has been applied to soften the final colours. Blue or vermilion form the background and the figures are outlined in contrasting colours.

Perhaps the most obvious form of folk art is the decoration found on the walls of temples and homes alike, an art which, alas, is fast disappearing. Mansions in Sikar between Jaipur and Bikaner, and others in Bundi and elsewhere, are lavishly adorned with murals depicting battles, hunting scenes, stories from the epics and fantastic animals. Imposing elephants complete with howdahs and princes, prancing horses bearing warriors and bridegrooms, soldiers, dancing girls, deities, all enliven the whitewashed walls of village homes, temples and family castles.

To celebrate weddings, hereditary artists called *chateras* execute another series of royal processions honouring bride and groom. As wealthier families tend to move to modern villas or apartments the craft is dying out in towns; but in the country, the women themselves keep the folk art alive. Using coloured rice paste in *mandana* patterns, they decorate household thresholds with such symbols as lotuses (the life force), a pair of feet – those of the goddess Lakshmi, indicating the entrance of prosperity – and Surya the sun-god from whom comes all life, and who is shown as a concentric swirl or a masculine figure.

34 The hair of this camel at Bikaner has been sheared into a beautiful and intricate pattern

CARPETS

Jaipur has a reputation for producing fine carpets and dhurries, the carpets usually in traditional Persian designs, introduced by the Mughals in the fifteenth century when Persian weavers were employed in the royal workshops. Today prisoners in local jails are trained in the art. Dhurries are cotton fabrics which can be simple floor coverings or, as in Jaisalmer and Jaipur, sophisticated patterned coverings for beds, screens and windows.

COSMETICS

A craft in itself is the classical Indian method of beautifying a woman, with the utensils usually of silver or brass. During the Gangaur festival girls decorate each other's hands with *mehndi*, a paste of myrtle leaves, producing henna, ground in water and mixed with lime juice. The delicate designs, each with its own significance, are used on hands and feet for various ceremonies but particularly weddings. The paste is dark brown when applied, but as it dries and is brushed off, it leaves a charming reddish-brown stain said to be cooling as well as decorative and the bringer of good fortune.

The *tika* or *bindi*, usually a vermilion spot on the forehead, is another mark of beauty that can vary enormously in style and design. Some historians believe it has its origins among the pre-Aryan inhabitants of India, possibly following the sacrifice of an animal, when its blood would be smeared on the deity's forehead. And since the invading Aryans believed that women were the incarnation of the Mother Goddess, an animal would be sacrificed at the time of a girl's marriage, on the threshold of her new home, and the bride herself would receive the ritual smear of blood on the forehead. Rajput brides today shape their *tikas* as a sun or a crescent moon, symbolizing eternal happiness with their husbands, and perhaps also indicating their legendary descent from the sun or the moon. Widows, having lost this happiness, no longer use the *tika* or any other form of ornamentation.

Eyes are emphasized by the use of *kajal* or *kohl*, not only to enhance their appearance but to ward off demons and contagious diseases. *Kajal* is the soot or *surmah* made by burning tightly-rolled cotton-wool in a small bowl of oil, trapping the soot into another small vessel inverted over the wick. Both vessels must be of silver or earthenware, and the oil may be mustard, castor or any other vegetable oil. The powder is mixed with a little clarified butter, or just used dry. The silver containers and slender wands used to apply the *kajal* are among the many lovely objects decorating an Indian woman's dressing-table; many are collectors' pieces with exquisite engraving and unusual shapes.

35 A *bhel* or *rath*, a bullock-drawn purdah cart, near Jaipur

CHAPTER FOUR
Melas –
The Fun of the Fair

The numerous Rajasthani festivals – *melas* – whether secular or religious, are dazzlingly theatrical and gay, an opportunity for villagers to forget everyday problems, to relax with old friends and catch up with the news through visitors from faraway places.

Biggest and most famous of all is the annual camel and cattle fair, held every November at Pushkar near Ajmer. The sacred lake of Pushkar is one of the five major places of Hindu pilgrimage in India. Peacocks and monkeys are venerated here, while the enormous fish and alligators are regularly fed by the priests whose temples skirt the lake.

Long ago, in the misty past, a demon called Vajranabh lived at Pushkar devouring the children of the god Brahma. Furious, Brahma slew the demon with a lotus he was holding in preparation for the Vedic fire rite of Yagna, and the petals floated to earth, falling in three places to create the three lakes of Pushkar. A misunderstanding between Brahma and his consort Saraswati (or Savitri), who was late attending the Yagna ceremony where her presence as his wife was vital, led to Brahma choosing a substitute in a pretty milkmaid, Gayatri. Eventually Saraswati was placated when temples were built in honour of all three. These temples are now objects of pilgrimage with as many as a thousand visitors daily, even in normal times.

Early visitors included the fifth-century Chinese traveller Fa-Hsien, and every Rajput prince built a palace along the edge of this, the most sacred lake in India; at one time the marble terraces were lined with temples, most of which were destroyed by Aurangzeb and other fanatical Muslim emperors. But the fifty-two ghats, flights of marble steps around the lake, still remain, many occupied by Vanshavalis, professional keepers of genealogies armed with fat exercise books filled with the names of past pilgrims. Visitors squat by a turbaned Vanshavali as he leafs through the books to find the names of their ancestors, recorded when they visited this holy place.

The scene on Kartik Purnima in November, when perhaps a hundred thousand people flock to commemorate Brahma's Yagni rites, begins at three in the morning with crowds queuing to bathe in the lake on this auspicious day. Once the many special religious ceremonies have been performed, the massive crowds make their way to the dusty plain behind the Brahma temple, transformed from its usual neglected isolation to an explosion of exotic hues and sounds. Hundreds of gaily canopied booths provide sticky sweetmeats, highly-spiced meatballs and curries, sherbets concocted from rose-petals; ivory bangles, votive offerings, toys, camel saddles and halters, glass beads, inlaid brassware and hand-printed cloth.

36 Sweetmeats on a stall at the Eklingji *mela*

Overleaf

37 Villagers walk many miles across the desert to the *mela* at Bairat

69

Wooden swings, merry-go-rounds and ferris wheels painted in gaudy stripes of scarlet, yellow, green and blue are besieged by eager throngs, while others watch wrestlers stripped to their loincloths, snake-charmers, acrobats and jugglers; minstrels recite ancient tales of chivalry; clapping to the rhythm of dancing girls and boys, many spectators struggle to puzzle the mystery of conjurers' tricks.

All this is but the overture to the real business of Pushkar, the splendid cattle fair, with its magnificent prize-winning Brahmani bulls adorned with garlands of marigolds, silver anklets and collars of jewels set in hammered silver, proudly displaying their awards. White racing camels, horses and even bullocks with painted horns are urged down the race-track.

But there are other, gentler celebrations such as the Raksha Bandhan, held on the day of the August full moon, when Rajput ladies tie a *rakhi* – a gold-trimmed silken bracelet – on the arms of their real or adopted brothers: a remembrance of the days of chivalry when women lacking male relatives often made such a gesture to a powerful chieftain or famous warrior who was then obliged to act as their protector. Generally the men so involved never even saw their adopted sisters, for the bracelet, which could range from a simple piece of silk or cord to an expensive jewelled armlet, was often sent through the offices of a priest. Often the *rakhi* involved a genuine plea for help, as in the case of the Rani Karnavati of Chitor, a Bundi princess whose baby son, Udai Singh, later to found the city of Udaipur, was smuggled to safety during the second sack of Chitor in 1533. The princess had sent a *rakhi* to the Mughal emperor Humayun, after which she herself led some 13,000 women and children to the funeral pyre, sooner than fall into the hands of the enemy. Humayun honoured the gesture by forcing the victorious attacker, the Sultan of Gujarat, to return the conquered fortress to the Sisodia family, rulers of Chitor.

Almost every temple festival is accompanied by a secular fair, but some have special peculiarities, such as the *mela* at the Ram Deoji shrine near Pokaran, between Jodhpur and Jaisalmer. Because of the saint's love of horses, toy horses are sold for temple offerings but the sale or consumption of meat or wine in the vicinity of the fair is forbidden; there are law-breakers, of course, but when caught they are heavily fined.

Ram Deoji has an added attraction in the performance of a *terah tali* by members of the Kamod community. Two men relate the history of Ram Deoji, accompanying themselves on a one-stringed instrument called an *ektara*. Meanwhile two women give an exhibition of acrobatic feats combined with depicting everyday tasks such as making butter and bread, harvesting crops, weaving; at the same time, they balance water-filled pots on their heads. Sometimes, to make the dance even more complicated, they perform with lighted candles in the pots, while heavy melons are tied to various parts of their bodies. The whole is a unique performance that can last the entire night.

Quite a different kind of *mela* is held at Sitabari in Kota, attracting as many as fifty thousand pilgrims to this densely forested area. The fair is associated with the Ramayana legend, when Sita was abandoned here in the forest and a stream of fresh water was miraculously created to quench her thirst. Hindus, Muslims and Harijans (untouchables) all come to the shrine built to mark Sita's banishment and to bathe in the waters of what are now four holy pools, which are said to cure mental disorders and whose waters, which never run dry, are always cool in summer and warm in winter.

Another fair, particularly popular with the Bhils, is held at Baneshwar in Udaipur. This is a joint *mela* celebrated by the temples of Vishnu and Shiva, when a silver image of Mavji, a local saint, is carried in procession. Bare-breasted unmarried Bhil tribal girls jostle the married girls, whose legs and arms are covered with ivory bangles. And at night, Bhil lads gather round bonfires to sing their tribal epics with high-pitched voices.

Another tribe, the Minas, celebrate their annual Benganga Fair at Bairat, site of the ancient Buddhist monastery and stupa where, in a Khejra tree (*Prosopis spicigera*), the Pandava brothers hid their bows and arrows before visiting the court of the local ruler. Palm trees surround the fairground, with low, rocky hills all around, and the Minas pay homage to the Mahabharata heroes with songs and dances.

Then there is the Gogaji *mela*, dedicated to an eleventh-century Rajput warrior revered in many guises, with a shrine in every Rajput village, also usually under a Khejra tree. His contemporary, Mahmud of Ghazni, was among his many Muslim admirers. Gogaji is represented in carvings on stones, as a warrior on horseback, and also as a snake; victims of snake-bite are carried to the village shrine and kept awake throughout the night by the beating of drums and gongs. At the fair itself, worshippers begin the day at Gogaji's memorial where the warrior is seen in the dress of a Chauhan ruler, a snake around his neck, and riding a blue horse. He holds a whip which is the object of much veneration, and most visitors carry bamboo poles with multicoloured flags, miniatures of the outsize flags flying on the shrine; meanwhile songs relating the long and complicated legend of Gogaji himself are sung to the accompaniment of gongs and drums.

Sacred peacocks feature at the shrine of Jambheswar (between Bikaner and Jodhpur) and many others, where pilgrims offer grain in vast quantities solely to feed the peacocks and other birds within the precincts.

Besides the scores of Hindu fairs others are held in connection with the Jain and Muslim religions. One of the biggest Jain *melas* is that of Shri Mahavir in Chandangaon (Sawai Madhopur district), held in memory of Shri Mahavir Swami, the twenty-fourth *tirthankar*, who lived in the sixth century before Christ. Pilgrims to his shrine come from as far away as Calcutta, Assam and Bihar, across the entire subcontinent. The image of Mahaviraj, buried deep under the ground, is said to have been discovered by the local cobbler several centuries ago. The cobbler was grazing his cattle at the spot where the shrine now stands, and his descendants play an essential role in the festivities when the image is carried in a gold chariot drawn by two bullocks to the banks of the nearby river. Peacock fans are waved over the statue and a male descendant of the original cobbler must push the chariot symbolically, or it is believed it will not move. Thousands of pilgrims escort the chariot, chanting, singing devotional songs, and competing for a garland worn by the statue while it is being submerged in the river, which is auctioned afterwards. Mina tribes accompany the chariot on its way to the river, then leave so that Gujars, with whom there was once a dispute, can escort the image back to the temple.

Typical of local fairs is the Urs at Nagaur near Bikaner, where ceremonies commemorating the death of the thirteenth-century Muslim Sufi saint, Khwaja Shah Hamiduddin Nagauri, are held within an enclosure entered through the immensely tall Atarkin's gateway of yellow sandstone. The gate, elaborately carved, with four white cupolas surmounting it, is almost concealed behind coloured garlands and striped canopies hung around the exterior to shelter stalls selling religious objects – rosaries and votive offerings – not to mention the beggars who take grateful advantage of the shade. An enormous *karwahad*, a veritable witches' cauldron permanently mounted atop a brick fireplace, cooks the meal prepared by a dozen men and women which is distributed freely among pilgrims.

Muslim festivals connected with shrines are generally strictly religious, but whether at the famous Dargah of Khwaja Muinuddin Chishti at Ajmer, the biggest Muslim fair in India, or smaller shrines such as that of Syed Fakhruddin of the Ismaili Shia Muslims in the remote village of Galiyakot in Bhil country, secular fairs with stalls, troubadours and swings outside the sacred areas entertain visitors of all creeds. In both Hindu and Muslim festivals food is prepared in vast quantities for free distribution, and two of the most spectacular containers for this purpose are those installed on twin pyramids of masonry just inside the Dargah of Muinuddin Chishti. The larger of the two, presented by the Emperor Akbar, is over three metres in diameter. The slighter smaller one was given by the Emperor Jahangir. During Urs and the gay festivals of Eid celebrating the birthday of the Prophet Muhammad or the end of the fasting period of Ramadan, the cauldrons are filled with a tasty mixture of rice, milk, sugar, clarified butter, nuts, spices and dry fruits donated by wealthy merchants and worshippers who include Hindus and Sikhs.

Then follows a ceremonial 'looting' when the shrine servants, specially dressed for the occasion, actually jump into the steaming rice mixture, called *kheer*, sometimes scalding themselves in the process, and within an hour have emptied the contents into bowls for the waiting crowds.

The Veerpuri Mela, an entirely secular August fair, commemorates the exploits of Rajput heroes and is held in the lovely gardens of Mandor on the outskirts of the city of Jodhpur. Here, in a delectable green oasis of magnificent shade-trees and flowering trees, pools, lawns and flowerbeds, like a vision of paradise to travellers from the surrounding arid desert, the seventeenth-century ruler of Jodhpur, Jaswant Singh, constructed a gallery carved from the rocky hillside. Sculptured from the rock are larger than life-size painted statues of warrior princes whose courageous exploits had inspired the prince to conquer an enemy greatly outnumbering his own forces. The hero Pabuji's black mare bears the signature of the historian Colonel James Tod, who confessed to having autographed the mare's hoof.

Something like sixty thousand people of all castes and creeds flock to the fair, when sisters place a vermilion mark on their brothers' foreheads and night-long sessions of poetry recitals are held in the gardens as families picnic under the trees. Traditional entertainment in the form of plays, minstrel songs, the recital of epics, and folk dances probably developed at

38 The *mela* at Triveni, near Bairat: bustling crowds among the tented stalls

the medieval courts of the princes when each vied with his neighbour to provide the finest performers. These days such diversions are mainly found at the larger festivals or, as in Udaipur and Jaipur, given new life and encouragement by performances before foreign and Indian guests at the one-time royal palaces, now converted to luxury hotels.

To watch the Pinguli puppets manipulated by master puppeteer Amer Singh, whose family have been making these string marionettes for at least four centuries, is to be transported into another world. The setting is perfect, a patio within the ethereal Lake Palace on Udaipur's Pichola Lake, with a stage where a score of puppets really performs to the accompaniment of *tabla* drums and descriptive songs and narration by the puppeteer's wife and young daughter. Warriors on horseback, emperors, queens, courtiers, jesters and dancing-girls vie with beautiful princesses and magicians producing flaming torches. The Rajasthani puppet theatre is known as Kaputli and some of the older stylized wooden puppets can be seen in stage settings in the folk museum in the old city.

Some of Rajasthan's most fascinating folk-dances are performed at night on the terraces of the Rambagh Palace, another former royal home converted to an hotel by the late Maharaja Jai Singh; here, where the Maharaja and his beautiful wife Gayatri (Ayesha) once entertained their friends with afternoon tea overlooking the peacock-studded lawns, Bhavais in typical tie-dyed scarlet and saffron *odhnis*, wide maroon skirts and arms covered with ivory bracelets now perform spectacular dances before hotel guests.

However, festivals are really where the indigenous dances are seen at their best. Round about Jodhpur and Bikaner the Kachi Ghori is performed only by men, riding hobby-horses and accompanied by large double *dhol* drums. Much loved by village women is the Ghummar, a circular dance in which the girls' whirling movements throw out their multicoloured petticoats as they sing. One especially spectacular dance is performed by the Sidhi Jats around Jaisalmer during the festival of Guru Jasnath, in March and April. The performers spin around and into huge bonfires, dancing across hot coals – not fire-walking but a real dance accompanied by flutes, pipes and drums.

Rajasthan is a country of hereditary minstrels and performers. Apart from the Bhavais who do the dance dramas and those described at Jaipur, Colonel Tod makes many references to the Charans and Bhats who were traditional carriers, allowed to transport goods between warring states with impunity, as well as being bards and genealogists, indispensable at royal weddings and other ceremonies. Charans mainly recite the genealogy of the royal families in verse form while the Bhats expound the classical epics. Among the most popular ballad singers are the Langas, who specialize in lyrical and satirical verses.

There is always some kind of festival in progress in Rajasthan; and those who mingle with the crowds share the excitement and emotion and find that the villagers will happily reveal their fascinating traditions.

39 The *pan* stall at a *mela*: the raw betel nut is wrapped in *pan* leaves spread with lime, and the packets then wrapped in silver foil

II
DHARMA
ABODE OF THE
SPIRIT

We have to learn yet that all religions,
under whatever name they may be called,
either Hindu, Buddhist,
Mohammedan or Christian,
have the same God,
and he who derides any one of these
derides his own God.
Swami Vivekananda

CHAPTER FIVE

The Religions

Travelling around Rajasthan one encounters a bewildering spectrum of beliefs represented by equally diverse objects including stones and trees. The countless carved stone phalluses, often with the female labia (the *lingam* and the *yoni*), together with the acrobatic coupling of deities exquisitely carved on temple walls, so shocking to earlier generations of visitors, are also aspects of a religion that can range from pure nature-worship to the most esoteric abstract thought. Most Rajputs are Hindus or Jains but there is a substantial Muslim population with important Islamic shrines. Understanding, however imperfectly, something of the religious beliefs held by these people adds to the fascination of travel.

As far as we can tell from the scanty clues given by archaeological finds, the earliest people here practised *ahimsa* or non-violence and worshipped trees, the Mother Goddess and the phallus. The present-day Jain and Hindu association of deities with various animals is a reminder of prehistoric cults; the bull was regarded as a fertility and lunar symbol in ancient Mesopotamia and Persia and may have been the prototype for the Nandi bulls facing most Shiva shrines.

In the mid-second millennium BC the Aryan invaders, who already worshipped deities personifying the powerful forces of nature, soon absorbed the Dravidian gods into their own religion. The oldest known written religious texts in the world are the Vedas, a word meaning knowledge, consisting of four huge collections of religious and traditional historic material composed by Aryan Brahman priests. The first of the Vedas (1,028 hymns dedicated to Aryan deities) was arranged and written early in the first millennium BC; two later Vedas contain priestly instructions, incantations and sacrificial formulae with a long appendix called the Brahmanas, probably written about 800 to 600 BC.

Hinduism, a marvellously fluid and adaptable religion, seems to have developed from this mixture of Dravidian and Aryan beliefs, with the introduction of the concept of a universal spirit in which every living thing was merely a manifestation of the One, Unchangeable, Absolute and Impersonal Being, Brahm or Brahma. Its teaching is adjusted according to the intellectual development of the individual.

The Supreme Being has three personal manifestations, Brahma the Creator, Vishnu the Preserver and Shiva the Destroyer. And since by withholding preservation one can destroy, and conversely, preserve by withholding destruction, Vishnu and Shiva, both capable of creation, become with Brahma an indivisible trinity.

All the gods have vehicles, real or mythical animals or birds, usually but

40 Images of Radha and Krishna in a small temple at Galta, near Jaipur

not always shown near or beneath the deity. All three gods have four arms, and Brahma the Creator (very rarely portrayed) has four heads, each of which rules a quarter of the universe. Brahma's vehicle is a goose, and in his four hands he holds a rosary, a spoon for lustral rites, a portion of the Veda and a vessel of lustral water. Unlike the remainder of the trinity, Brahma has no incarnations, but like them he does have a *shakti*, the female force complementing his power. Brahma's *shakti* is Saraswati or Savitri, goddess of learning and the arts; she rides a peacock or a swan and plays the *vina*, a type of lute. Because of his comparatively nebulous aspect, Brahma has relatively few followers, and fewer temples are dedicated to him; the most important of these is at Pushkar.

The other gods, with their many aspects, are more difficult to recognize. Shiva the Destroyer is in fact most usually found in his creative aspect, symbolized by the phallus or *lingam*. Where he is depicted in manlike form, as teacher of music, yoga and all wisdom, he wears a tiger-skin round his loins and in his four hands he holds a battle-axe, a trident, a drum and an antelope skin or a cobra, symbols of solitary meditation in the forests. You will also see him as Nataraj, the Cosmic Dancer, portrayed with tremendous vigour as he dances in a halo of flames.

In his truly destructive aspect, Shiva is Chaumunda or Bhairava, wearing a garland of skulls and lurking in cemeteries and on battlefields, personifying death as the generator of life. Among his many other forms Shiva is worshipped as Mahadeo, the Great God, and his vehicle, Nandi the bull with the gentle face and soft eyes, keeps watch before his temples.

Often the entrance is guarded by Shiva's elephant-headed son, Ganesha, the most auspicious of all the gods, patron of writers and artists and the epitome of wisdom, usually with a mouse or a rat at his feet. Ganesha was the elder of Shiva and Parvati's two sons (Karttikeya, god of war, was the younger); the story goes that Shiva, in a temper, cut off his son's head. Later, remorseful, he vowed that he would replace it with the head of the first living creature to pass by, which happened to be an elephant!

Shiva's consort Parvati is the powerful goddess of beauty and a development from the Dravidian Mother Goddess, with several different aspects. She can be Gauri the charming, faithful, eternally happy wife; the black side of her nature is Kali, the terrible ebony goddess with her garland of human skulls, demanding propitiation by sacrifice – which until recently was often human. She is also Durga, the goddess of war, with ten arms to wield her awful weapons. Quite often she is symbolized merely as the female genitalia, the *yoni*, together with Shiva's *lingam*. Shiva's followers practise penances and are often students of the psychic control of tantrism.

Vishnu, by contrast, is a mild and compassionate deity who probably evolved from one of the Vedic sun gods. He is usually shown wearing a tall jewelled crown and, as a warrior who is the protector and preserver of the universe, holds in his four hands the weapons of war: the sharp-edged discus, a sword, the conch-shell used as a war-trumpet, and a long club. Sometimes he is seated with his wife Lakshmi, goddess of wealth and beauty, on the serpent Sheesh, symbol of eternity, while Brahma on a lotus blossom springs from his navel. Vishnu in fact has two consorts: Bhudevi, the earth goddess, is his second partner and is usually shown standing on his left.

41 Wayside Shiva shrine, partially painted the sacred red colour, near Ranthambhor

Vishnu's vehicle is the Garuda, mythical half-man, half-bird. And to add to the confusion for the non-Hindu, Vishnu is also shown as one of the nine incarnations in which he appeared on earth, for at the end of each great cycle of time the earth is destroyed. In each cycle, Vishnu appears as saviour of the world, incarnations which have included a boar, fish, tortoise, lion, horse and dwarf. As a compromise to Buddhism, his most recent incarnation was as Lord Buddha himself.

The most popular forms in which Vishnu is worshipped are those of Rama and Krishna. Rama is the hero of the Ramayana epic and may have been an actual chief of the eighth or seventh century BC, although he was not included in the Ramayana legend until the first century BC. He is the embodiment of the ideal husband, son, and brother, while his wife Sita is the ideal Indian woman. Their ally Hanuman the monkey god, epitome of the faithful, devoted servant, often stands guard at the entrance to fortresses, and monkeys are treated with respect all over India, whatever their pranks.

Krishna, a handsome youth, always portrayed with a dark blue skin which may point to a Dravidian origin, is the hero of the earlier Mahabharata epic. He was a light-hearted, amorous pastoral god, charming animals and humans alike, fond of playing the flute and dancing with milkmaids and shepherdesses. But he had a more serious side, coming to the aid of the Pandava brothers in their battles, as related in the Bhagavad Gita, 'the most exalted and beautiful' of all India's religious poems, expressing, for the first time, the love of God for man, and forming the ethical basis of modern Hinduism.

This is an extremely brief outline of the main Hindu deities but there are scores of others, all manifestations of the Supreme Spirit, making for a bewildering array of images confronting the traveller. Even this superficial sketch of Hinduism demonstrates how wide is its range of beliefs.

Literally hundreds of simple, animistic shrines are to be seen in Rajasthan, mainly strikingly-shaped stones *(murti)*, rather like modern abstract sculpture, which have been covered with vermilion *(sindura)*, the sacred colour, and adorned with silver and coloured paper and flowers, real and artificial. Tribal people and simple village folk still revere many of the old nature gods, although they may give them more conventional titles. The cult of rudimentary carved or naturally shaped stones probably originally suggested a sacred force associated with healing powers.

One of the most interesting of ancient practices is that of tree-worship, which can be of actual living trees or symbolic images of the Tree of Life – the Kalpa-vriksha. The peepul or bo tree (a type of wild fig, *Ficus religiosa*) has been regarded as sacred since the Harappan period; it is associated with Vishnu and was also the tree under which the Buddha found enlightenment. Ancient burial grounds are often found among groves of banyan *(Ficus indica)*, whose aerial roots, suspended from the main branches, reach down to the ground. This tree is especially sacred to followers of Shiva who see in its tangled roots a resemblance to Shiva's ascetic aspect when he grew his hair in long, unkempt locks.

Jan Pieper in 'Arboreal Art and Architecture in India' gives a fascinating study of Kalpa-vriksha, the abundance-granting tree of paradise depicted in ancient carvings. Many of these date from Ashoka's time and are in the form

With his limbs, tender and dark like rows of clumps of blue lotus flowers,
By herd-girls surrounded, who embrace at pleasure any part of his body,
Friend, in spring, beautiful Hari (Krishna) plays like love's own self
Conducting the love-sport, with love for all, bringing delight into being.

Jayadeva

42 Eighteenth-century fresco at Bundi: Krishna dallying with the *gopis* (herd-girls)

of *stambhas* or monolithic pillars crowned with a tree. The Kalpa-vriksha was one of five trees found in Indra's paradise, located in the centre of the earth, and the stone tree represented the concept of order and beauty, apart from the more universal idea of the life force associated with water and perpetual rejuvenation.

In India, all trees are treated with respect and veneration. Since they retain ground water during long droughts, the wells dug close by are often the only sources of water at such times. The *chhatri* or umbrella, symbol of royalty which crowns the Buddhist stupas, may be derived from the custom of the ruler sitting in the shade of a sacred tree, and there are numerous examples of sacred trees being converted into places of worship, with brick or stone platforms built around them; they also serve as resting-places for pilgrims and meeting-centres for village elders. Such a tree often blocks a main road, which will be divided to preserve the tree *in situ*.

An unusual Kalpa-vriksha surmounts the Chintamani Pashunath Swamiji Jain temple among the sand-buried ruins of Lodurva, original capital of Jaisalmer. Fashioned of various metals, the mass of branches and leaves bears all kinds of fruits and the whole is enclosed within a protective cage. Jaisalmer itself is one of the great Jain centres of Rajasthan and the religion is based on ideas that were in circulation in the seventh century BC.

Vardhamana, the twenty-fourth and last of the *tirthankars* ('perfect souls' or 'ford-makers'), was the virtual founder of Jainism, born about 599 BC to Raja Siddartha, head of a warrior clan in Bihar, north-eastern India. His mother was a daughter of a ruling monarch and the prince earned a reputation for his courage and heroic deeds. He married and had one daughter but when he was thirty his parents died and instead of taking his father's place as Raja, he renounced his family, joined the Parsvanatha monastic order and for the next twelve years wandered through the country as a religious mendicant, subjecting his body to innumerable hardships. For the first eighteen months he wore a single garment which he never changed. Then he discarded it and spent the rest of his life entirely nude, with no possessions at all. This is why many Jain statues are represented nude.

Finally Vardhamana was recognized as a *jina* (spiritual conqueror), and given the title of 'Mahavira' (Great Hero) by which he is generally known today.

Mahavira's teachings were those of his predecessors, that is, the attainment of salvation through rebirth and asceticism. To gain release from the cycle of reincarnation, Jains practise three main principles, the 'Triple Jewel': Right Belief, Right Knowledge – the correct understanding of the Jain theory of the world, maintaining that every individual person or thing has a soul – and Right Conduct.

These in turn are divided into five vows, the first of which is non-violence *(ahimsa)* – very strict Jains wear a fine linen mask over their mouths and noses, to avoid breathing in some small insect, and sweep the ground before them lest they accidentally tread on an ant. The other vows are to tell the truth, not to steal, and not to become attached to possessions; the fifth, added by Mahavira himself, is celibacy or Brahmacharya, the triumph over passions of all kinds. When he was seventy-two, Mahavira starved himself to death. During the following centuries Jain teachings were handed down

43 A peacock on the Harihara temple, one of the complex at Osian built between the eighth and eleventh centuries

Overleaf

44 A silver-covered deity in the Hall of Heroes at the Mandor Gardens, Jodhpur

45 Durgadevi with the black and white Bhairons, aspects of Shiva, at the Harshanath folk temple near Sikar. The figures have been completely covered in vermilion powder *(sindura)* by priests as a mark of respect *(top left)*. See p. 127

46 The central Shiva image in the Sammidhesvara temple at Chitor *(top right)*

47 A deity covered with hundreds of layers of silver foil by worshippers, in a small shrine on the wall of the Bikaner City Palace *(bottom left)*

48 The silver door to the Karni Mata temple at Deshnoke: relief of the goddess with her rats *(bottom right)*

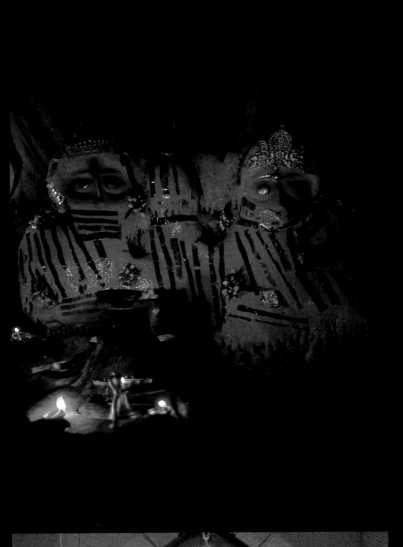

orally, but about the third century BC they were collected and recorded, and a final version was produced in the fifth century AD.

The monastic order established by Mahavira consisted of four classes – monks, nuns, lay-brothers and lay-sisters. It was on a point of monastic discipline that a schism arose in the first century, resulting in the Digambaras, 'sky-clad' or naked, following literally the example of Mahavira, and the Svetambaras who wore white or yellow robes. Although there was no real difference in their fundamental doctrines, the Svetambaras were great collectors of sacred books, and thanks to their love of literature and the belief that to copy even a secular manuscript was to perform a work of religious merit, many rare texts have been preserved to this day.

Jains do not worship a deity, for they believe that the universe functions according to an eternal law, and that it suffers continual change as it passes through a series of cosmic waves of progress and decline. These cycles each contain twenty-four *tirthankars* and twelve Universal Emperors (Chakra-vartins) who live at regular intervals in the cycles. At the peak period men are of gigantic size and survive to a tremendous age, needing no laws or property, for the amazing Kalpa-vriksha gives them all they need. Our present age is one of decline which will continue for forty thousand years, by which time men will have been reduced to dwarf-like stature and live in caves, having forgotten all culture, including the use of fire, and with a lifespan of only twenty years. After this, the period of improvement will begin, but this cycle of decline and progress will last for eternity.

Women and laymen can never attain Nirvana, that blissful freedom from rebirth. And a monk can only achieve it by sacrificing all earthly ties, including clothes, and by a long course of fasting and self-mortification. However, very few monastic orders practise nudity or self-inflicted torture today.

This rather grim picture of Jainism hardly presents a true portrait of the majority of secular Jains. Generally speaking a wealthy, commercial community, they are noted for their charitable efforts including the maintenance of hospitals, schools and colleges and *pinjrapols* or hospitals for sick animals.

Through the ages the religion has attracted the rich trading community, who specialize in bartering goods and act as middle-men in financial transactions, thus avoiding any occupation endangering the life of other creatures. This affluent Jain community, the Marwari merchants, has been responsible for building the magnificent temples that abound in Rajasthan, especially at Mount Abu and Ranakpur. And while their secular rites at weddings and funerals are the same as those of the Hindus, their temples have gradually become repositories for statues of the *tirthankars*.

Very often the chief Hindu gods have also found niches in these temples, for Jains are tolerant of all religions. Early Jainism had much in common with its contemporary, Buddhism, but while Jainism has survived and flourishes, only a few ruins remind us that Buddhism ever existed here. Both religions were founded by young men of royal blood and warrior caste, opposed to the authority of the Vedas, and to the practice of animal sacrifice; both men became wandering mendicants when about thirty years old and both attracted the lower classes of society as well as the high-born.

49 The entrance of the Karni Mata temple at Deshnoke

Buddha was born Prince Siddartha about 565 BC (or, according to the Mahabodhi Society, he lived from 624 BC to 544 BC), and his father ruled a small kingdom which is now part of southern Nepal. After spending his boyhood in the luxury of a royal court, he wandered about his father's capital in disguise, seeing for himself the misery of the poor and the sick. He married, dutifully siring a son, and then abandoned his wife and family and life of ease to become a religious mendicant like Mahavira, practising severe austerities until finally, after spending some time in contemplation under a Bo tree, he received enlightenment – his title of Buddha means 'the enlightened one'.

By now Buddha had given up the self-torture he originally practised, denouncing such extremes, but preached instead an eightfold path, the middle path between worldliness and asceticism. Buddhists believe that every living thing is doomed to destruction and the only way man can avoid constant reincarnation is to renounce all earthly things. However, good deeds enable a Buddhist to pass to a higher scale of development in the cycle of rebirth. Like the Jain teacher, Buddha believed that the greatest possible bliss was Nirvana, to be attained only by suppressing all sensual passions. Unlike Jainism, Buddhism teaches that everyone, regardless of caste, is capable of reaching Nirvana by strictly following the eightfold Noble Path of Right Views, Right Aspirations, Right Speech, Right Conduct, Right Living, Right Effort, Right-Mindedness and Right Meditation.

Buddha gathered a number of followers, founded a monastic order accepting both men and women of all strata of society and, with his monks, wandered about the country preaching his new religion. He is said to have died at the age of eighty, when his body was cremated and the ashes divided among various tribal people and his followers. In time stupas or tumuli were built over the ashes and temples or shrine rooms came later, at the beginning of the Christian era, when the image of Buddha began to be revered.

The Buddhist canon was not collected until some five hundred years after his death, and underwent many changes, incorporating the interpolations of his disciples. As with Jainism, Brahmans supervised births, marriages and deaths, but gradually Buddhism lost its individuality in Northern India and became instead a rather unorthodox Hindu sect. It did not survive the Muslim invasion here, when its great monasteries were sacked, libraries burnt, and monks slaughtered – most of the survivors fleeing to the Himalayas for refuge. But the religion did have a lasting influence on both Jainism and Hinduism.

The new, austere religion of Islam – literally 'submission to God' – arrived effectively in India from Afghanistan with the Ghaznavid invasion in 1001 AD, although there had been an Arab incursion in the early eighth century, on the coast near present-day Karachi. But it was in 1192 that another Muslim warrior from Afghanistan, Muhammad of Ghor, defeated the Rajput hero Prithviraj of Delhi and conquered Ajmer, establishing a Muslim base in the heart of Rajasthan. The considerable Muslim population of Rajasthan, thirty to forty per cent in some areas, dates from that period.

The founder of this strictly monotheistic religion was Muhammad, 'the Praised', who was born at Mecca in 570 AD into the ruling tribe of the Quraysh, claiming direct descent from Abraham.

50 The entrance to the Adhai-din-ka Jhonpra, the 'two-and-a-half-day mosque', at Ajmer

When he was twenty-five, Muhammad became the manager of a merchant caravan business owned by a wealthy widow, Khadija, fifteen years his senior. The widow proposed marriage and the couple had several sons, all of whom died in infancy, and four daughters, three of whom survived. Every year during the hot weather Muhammad retreated with his family to a cave on nearby Mount Hira. It was here, when he was forty, that the first divine revelations were made to Muhammad, when the angel Gabriel commanded him to spread a new religion. Persecuted for his teachings, his wife and uncle (his guardian) now dead, Muhammad became destitute. After threats to his life he left Mecca in 622, with an old friend, Abu Bakr, and Omar, who had been one of his fiercest opponents, on what is now known as the Hegira (Flight), from which the Muslim era is dated.

Settling at the rival city of Yathreb, some 270 km north of Mecca, he was accepted as a true prophet, and the city's name was changed to Medinat-un-Nabi, or Medina, 'The City of the Prophet'. The people of Mecca, meanwhile, had followed him, launching unsuccessful attacks against him and the Medinans, and in 630, Muhammad turned to the attack himself, leading a force of ten thousand to conquer Mecca. Returning to Medina, he died there two years later and was buried in the city.

The fundamental principle of Muhammad's teaching was simple: One God, One Prophet, One Book (the Koran), embodying the teachings and precepts of the Prophet. The religion allows 'no graven images'; hence the early fanatical Muslims made a point of mutilating or destroying all carvings and paintings portraying human or animal figures, and this resulted in devastating destruction of many ornate temples. There is a fatalistic acceptance of God's Will, equality of all believers, a caste-free society and the command to wage a holy war on all unbelievers who refuse to accept the new religion when given the opportunity.

Muslims must perform four main duties: prayers five times daily, after ablutions; the giving of alms; keeping the fast of Ramadan for a month, and, at least once in a lifetime, making the pilgrimage (the Haj) to Mecca. Devout Muslims are strict non-smokers and teetotallers, do not eat pork, play games of chance or practise usury. Today they are divided into two main sects, the Sunnis and the Shias, disagreeing over the leadership of Islam, and most Indian Muslims are Sunnis.

Although the Prophet allowed a man to have up to four wives, largely to afford protection to the many women and girls widowed or orphaned through constant warfare, he made the proviso that this was only permitted provided that the man could guarantee to treat each wife exactly the same. It was also considered sinful for a man to look upon the face of any woman other than a near relative, hence the introduction of purdah into India where, until the Muslim invasion, women had never been veiled or kept in strict seclusion.

The tolerance shown by the Mughal emperors, whose Rajput wives were allowed to observe their own Hindu religion, was an encouraging change from the widespread religious fanaticism in other countries, and is manifest today in many of the mosques and shrines of Rajasthan where Hindus, Sikhs and Muslims join to pay their respects to saintly men and women of all faiths.

51 Monkeys on the small Krishna temple at Galta, near Jaipur. Through the arch behind them is a fresco of Krishna and the *gopis*

CHAPTER SIX
Sacred Festivals

Twilight falls swiftly in India, and the setting sun casts long shadows over Nathdwara, 'The Portal of the God', a quaint little town on the road between Udaipur and Jodhpur.

Hidden in its narrow, twisting medieval streets is a great temple dedicated to Srinathji, Lord Krishna: a place so holy that it is one of the rare temples where non-Hindus are forbidden to set foot, even within the outer courtyard. It is also the object of fervent pilgrimages, but on a late April evening it was no pilgrimage that accounted for the excited and colourful crowds. It was the Gangaur festival, the most important as well as one of the most entrancing and distinctively Rajput of all, and it follows the gay Holi celebrations of spring.

'Gan' is another name for Lord Shiva, while 'Gaur' or 'Gauri' is perhaps better known as Shiva's consort, Parvati, symbolizing married bliss and fidelity. It is Gauri who is said to be the real creator of the world, the eternal Mother of the Cosmos, dedicated to the service of her Lord. No wonder that Gangaur is a favourite with women, both would-be brides and married women. Even Gan takes a back seat on this occasion.

Wooden images of Gauri and sometimes of her consort are specially carved for the occasion, some of them over a metre in height and others no bigger than small dolls. Every one is carefully arrayed in elaborate robes and 'jewels' – genuine in the case of wealthy families, otherwise imitation, which takes hours of preparation, the women kneading gram flour into dough and artistically moulding the 'jewellery' which they colour with rice paste.

The crowds in Nathdwara lined the sloping path to Moti Mahal, the great mansion on a hill, home of the chief priest of the Srinathji temples. A low wall along the road provided a somewhat perilous grandstand for the procession below, and an eager crowd of Bhils, the men with their distinctive flat white turbans edged with a dark ochre band, and the women in calf-length, patterned skirts and deep crimson *odhni* veils, hung over the long wall like so many animated sacks.

Announced by the trumpeting of the town band, every man in it wearing a sugar-pink turban, the head of the procession appeared in a twist of the narrow street some ten or fifteen metres below the wall. Horses with saddle-cloths trimmed in sugar-pink and silver danced in step to the music. Escorts in white shirts and *dhotis*, sugar-pink turbans and sashes, walked by the side of the horses, followed by covered palanquins and finally by the pink-clad Gauri herself, carried in the arms of an attendant walking beside the empty but most elaborate palanquin.

Nathdwara is noted for the fact that on each of the seven days of procession a different colour scheme is chosen for all the participants, who

52 The Mahavira Jain temple in the Osian group was begun in the eighth century. It is considered one of the most perfect monuments of the period, although it has been vandalized. The Jain nun is wearing a mask to protect her from accidentally ingesting insects

Overleaf

53 An attendant washing the altar of the Neminath Sandeshwar Jain temple at Bikaner. *See p. 120*

54 In a small Ganesha temple near Bikaner, the image of the god wears a tutu, while the *pujari* (priest) performs a ceremony. *See p. 120*

receive their costumes free from the Town Council. On the final day, Gauri is dressed in a black veil bordered with gold lace, a colour scheme copied by the women who follow with their individual Gauris.

After the procession, the crowd split up, some to make for the temple behind the mass of small shops selling religious mementoes; an open space is blocked at one end by a high wall on which are depicted two enormous and splendid blue elephants and their mahouts, flanking the entrance to an inner courtyard guarded by an armed soldier. This is as far as a non-Hindu is allowed, but one can glimpse a pair of magnificent silver doors leading to the temple itself.

In the sanctuary stands the unique, powerful black marble image of Lord Krishna, his eyes wide and staring, his feet turned out at right angles. His robes and ornaments are changed six times daily: the god is depicted first as a child, then a pastoral deity playing his flute in the forest of Brindavan; next as the gay lover, flirting with herd girls; then as a king, a philosopher and finally, at the end of the day, as Srinath, the Divine Lord, covered with pink lotuses and fabulous jewels which form part of the immense temple treasure. Hundreds of devotees crowd the temple daily for the privilege of these glimpses (known as *jhankis*) of their Lord Krishna.

The Srinath temple, built very simply of brick and limestone, is not only one of the holiest in Northern India but one of the wealthiest. It contains immense storerooms of rice and flour, pits filled with milk, and various other comestibles. Some twenty thousand cows are milked daily, while the income from a number of villages is donated to provide the free meals for worshippers. Two thousand people are engaged in doing nothing but keeping accounts and administering the meals.

Leaving Nathdwara for Udaipur, do make a point of visiting another extremely sacred complex at Eklingji, nestling in a thickly-wooded defile about twenty kilometres north of Udaipur. Eklingji is a little village where Bappa Rawal, the eighth-century founder of the Mewar dynasty, met a hermit called Harit who possessed a singularly powerful *lingam* image. The prince's prayers to the image enabled him to capture the fortress of Chitor and he built the first temple here to commemorate the event; his statue can be seen in the courtyard. There are as many as a hundred and eight temples within the high walls by the side of a lake. In spite of its sanctity there are no objections to a non-Hindu visitor, provided shoes and socks are removed; however, photography is absolutely forbidden.

There is a story that when the Muslim Sultan of Delhi, Alauddin Khilji, first attacked Mewar in 1295, he made straight for this sacred complex, intending to destroy it. As he entered the courtyard he passed a huge bronze statue of Nandi the bull, and struck at it with his sword. A swarm of angry bees poured from the hollow image and attacked the Sultan, who fled from the scene, taking this as an omen that perhaps it would be prudent to leave this particular shrine unharmed.

The bronze statue, with another of black marble, still faces the white marble shrine, which is fronted by a low enclosure divided in two, women sitting in the front portion, facing the sanctuary, and men behind. During festivals an unending queue winds round this enclosure to pass in front of the silver sanctuary with its unusual four-faced black marble image of

55 A sweeper in the Govind Devji temple at Jaipur. She is piously wearing the discarded jasmine garlands which had earlier been offered by worshippers in the temple

Overleaf

56 A *sadhu* – a holy man or wandering ascetic – in red robes, Jaipur

57 At the Eklingji *mela*, a wandering ascetic impersonating Lord Shiva *(top left)*

58 An itinerant *sadhu* at Jodhpur *(top right)*

59 A *sadhu* at Erinpura. He had taken a vow never to stop moving, and as he was talking to us his legs and arms were constantly in motion. He said he never stopped even when asleep *(bottom left)*

60 A Muslim dervish dancing in an ecstatic trance at the Dargah of Muinuddin Chishti, Ajmer *(bottom right)*

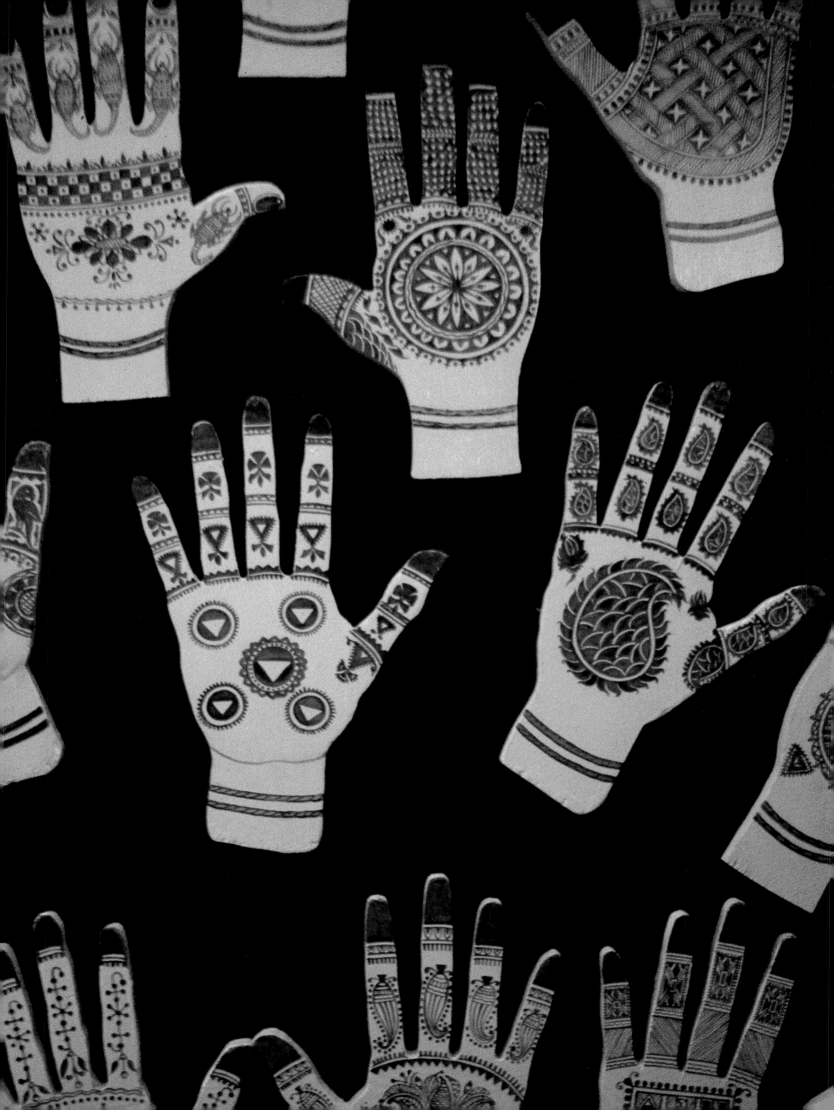

Mahadeva Shiva. Worshippers proffer garlands and small sums of money and are rewarded with blessings, a handful of sacred rosewater and a saffron *tika* on their foreheads.

During the Gangaur functions, life-sized garlanded Gauri images are carried through the town and placed facing the white marble shrine. To one side of the pillared hall, a choir of small boys in saffron caps and shirts chant hymns, for all the world like a cathedral choir. And, like choirboys anywhere, they drop their gravity as soon as the service ends and they file into the courtyard to join the other children playing round the many temples.

Outside this main shrine, where formerly the rulers of Mewar would seek the blessings of Mahadeva before embarking on any new venture, cluster other buildings, some no more than a small cell, but each with its attendant priest, and its image. They include an elegant Vishnu temple dedicated by the mystic princess Mirabai, with an eagle-headed *garuda* at the entrance. Galleries of smaller shrines include one to Ambika the earth deity, with a lion and elephant-headed Ganesha guarding one corner, and steps leading down to a cavern with an underground spring and the *lingam-yoni* symbols of Lord Shiva. This is the most ancient part of the complex and it is said to have been the very residence of the hermit Harit.

With some local variations, Gangaur is celebrated all over Rajasthan. In the early mornings of the eighteen-day festival, groups of women gather at the nearest lake carrying many pots, each smaller than the last, on their heads. The pots are filled with flowers, water and green grasses, which they throw into the water. Later in the morning they carry images of the goddess throughout the streets, singing different songs for every stage of the festivity, during which the girls decorate each other's hands and feet with a henna dye in intricate patterns, invoking future happiness and prosperity.

For most married women, Gangaur is the opportunity to take a holiday and visit their parents' home. A special song for this has the wife begging her husband to let her make the visit, the husband reluctant to part with her, and finally relenting. This is followed by another song asking the husband to provide the finest jewellery possible, so that his wife may honour the goddess with her appearance.

Many myths and legends have grown up around Gangaur and one of these, Ghudlia, recalls an historical incident when, in 1491, a hundred and forty maidens celebrating Gangaur were abducted by a Mir Ghudley Khan. Mir Ghudley was killed when the ruler of Jodhpur rescued the captured girls. Today, unmarried girls buy specially made earthenware vessels pierced with many holes, and place candles or small oil lamps inside. They then walk from house to house on the seventh evening after the Holi festival, singing the song of Ghudley and his infamy, while householders give the girls refreshments and oil for their lamps.

The grand climax of Gangaur is best experienced in Udaipur, long famed for its lavish festivities and described in detail by Colonel Tod in his *Annals and Antiquities of Rajasthan*. The scale of celebrations has been reduced since the abolition of the princes but the excitement and spectacle remain. At sunset the narrow lanes of the old city fill with groups of women in a brilliant kaleidoscope of scarlet, yellow, green, purple, azure, and pink, lavishly

61 In the crafts museum at Udaipur, different *mehndi* (henna paste) designs for decorating the palms, to bring good fortune

decorated with gold or silver, each group headed by women carrying tall images of Gauri on their heads. Finally, carried shoulder-high through the old Tripolia or triple gateway and down the marble steps leading to the lakeside, come a dozen or more Gauris, the last rays of the sun mingling with purple shadows among the turreted palaces lining the lake, and picking out sparkling gems and glittering tinsel.

In earlier days *pakhals*, large leather containers carried on the backs of bullocks, were filled with *asha*, the powerful Rajput alcoholic drink, all provided by the ruler. For a vivid description, read Colonel Tod again.

Only Bundi State has ignored Gangaur since 1706, when the ruler's brother was drowned in the Chambal river while celebrating the festival in a boat with his wife and friends. A rogue elephant plunged into the river, upsetting the boat and drowning the entire party, bringing the festivities to an abrupt and permanent end.

Tribal peoples have their own special way of celebrating Gangaur, village communities carrying their Gauris from one settlement to another. Tribal boys and girls, who have a much more liberal existence than those of conventional Hindu families, make the Gangaur festival an opportunity for elopement, when such an action is considered as binding as marriage, and no further ceremony is necessary.

There are many other Hindu festivals – Holi, which precedes Gangaur, is noted for the coloured water participants spray over each other, and old clothes are recommended for this particular holiday! Then there is Diwali, the festival of lights, dedicated to Lakshmi, goddess of good fortune, when every dwelling and public building is outlined with flickering oil lamps in fairy-tale fashion, celebrating the return of Prince Rama and his wife Sita to their capital of Ayodhya. This is the time when account books are balanced for the year; it is also a period when, no matter what views are held on gambling, everyone joins in games of chance.

Before Diwali comes Dussehra, again a festival celebrated all over India but with a special significance for Rajputs, those great warriors who at this time pay homage to Durga, the goddess of battle and one of Parvati's many aspects. The Dussehra festival is usually observed during ten days of theatrical performances, often in the open air, and during the evening companies of touring actors portray the principal episodes in the Ramayana, ending with the burning of enormous effigies of the demon king, Ravan, and his brother, filled with firecrackers to make a spectacular climax to the plays.

In Rajasthan, besides the series of plays, ceremonies are held where weapons of war, horses and war-elephants are consecrated and dedicated anew to Durga in the religious rituals, until recently presided over by the Rajput princes and their family priests. Just before Partition, one of the last great Dussehra ceremonies took place in Gwalior, once part of Rajasthan but now a neighbouring state. For the previous nine days various religious services had included the sacrifice of a buffalo or a ram, and the distribution of free food to priests and worshippers. The day before Dussehra, the royal elephants were adorned with intricately-painted patterns on faces and trunks, their toenails polished and painted with gold leaf. And on the morning of the ceremony they were decked with elephant-sized jewellery, the genuine article, together with brocade and velvet trappings trimmed

62 A shrine to Hanuman, the monkey god, at the Bairat *mela*

with gold and silver. Horses too were painted with auspicious henna spots, their necks hung with jewelled collars and their backs covered with magnificent caparisons. Gold and silver howdahs on the elephants' backs carried the noblemen of the Scindia court, clad in traditional eighteenth-century court dress. The distinctive Scindia headgear of crescent-shaped turbans was decorated with jewels, while jewelled scabbards held the ancestral swords.

One solitary elephant carried an incongruous-looking party of Europeans in grey cutaway morning-suits, complete with top hats. These were members of an Italian family whose ancestors had commanded Scindia troops in battle several centuries earlier, and had been rewarded with lands and titles in Gwalior. The family had settled here, but had always brought their brides from Italy and worn their own European dress, even in traditional formalities at court.

The procession filed into the courtyard of the City Palace where His Highness, the late Maharaja George (after his royal godfather, King George V of Great Britain) Scindia, also clad in his eighteenth-century costume, his turban dripping with the fabulous Scindia pearls and emeralds, sat on the marble *gadi* overlooking the paved square. Then came the dedication, with magnificent horses saluting the ruler by kneeling before him, and the elephants majestically raising their trunks to trumpet a royal salute.

Her Highness the Maharani Vijaya Lakshmi took the principal part in a ritual held in the seclusion of the harem, with the wives of the noblemen. For this occasion only, the Maharani wore the old-style martial sari with one end brought up between the legs to form a divided skirt, a reminder of the time when the Maharanis rode into battle by the side of their husbands. She then danced before an image of the goddess Durga, holding flat dishes with lighted candles in each hand, and circling these around her head as she danced. Good fortune for the coming year depended on her keeping the candles alight!

Presentation of *nazar* followed – a tribute of gold coins by nobles to their ruler who would touch them and return them to the donor, sometimes with a gift of robes of honour. This was followed by a sumptuous banquet and royal entertainment. But the very next year the costly elephant stables were disbanded and it was the last time that the martial aspect of Dussehra was observed in Gwalior.

A religious festival of special significance to Rajasthan is that of Teej, another dedicated to Parvati, for this commemorated the day when she was finally united with her beloved Lord Shiva. This occurs in August when the monsoon rains have quenched the thirsty earth, baked hard during the long hot summer. At once the deserts bloom, the air is fresh and every suitable tree suddenly sprouts a swing, the younger women competing with each other to swing highest and closest to heaven. Everyone wears red clothing – in Jaipur the Maharaja used to present all his chieftains with red robes and fathers would give their daughters new red outfits.

The elaborately robed figure of Parvati, seated on a swing, would be carried before the Jaipur ruler and his nobles by teams of women singing hymns in honour of the goddess. On this auspicious festival when Parvati is said to have promised to grant all requests to petitioners, farmers take the

63 Sunset: in the main square of Jaipur, the flower-stall does a brisk trade in offerings for the temple

opportunity to claim ownership of abandoned land or houses.

Another ancient festival, perhaps dating to Scythian custom, is that of ancestor worship. Fifteen days at the end of the rainy season are devoted to this, particularly in Udaipur where the ruler would visit his family cenotaphs at Ahar, just outside the city. Here he would pray, and place garlands on each of the marble *chhatris*.

In the midst of many Hindu festivals come Muslim celebrations, some shrines attracting thousands of Muslim pilgrims from all over Islam. The anniversaries of the death of such saints as Sheikh Muinuddin Chishti at Ajmer, and one of his chief disciples, the Sufi saint Khwaja Shah Hamiduddin Nagauri at the Tarkashin or Atarkin shrine in Nagaur, are occasions for a great influx of Muslims.

Biggest of all the Rajasthan Muslim festivals is the six-day Urs commemorating the death of Chishti, with Hindus as well as Muslims participating. On the first morning, at five o'clock, a white flag is hoisted over the tomb by a direct descendant of the Chishti saint, the Sajjada Nashin. Four days later, at the same hour, the Jannati Gateway, 'Gateway to Heaven', is flung open for the only time in the year; the belief is that anyone passing through this gate seven times will be sure of having the gates of heaven opened to him.

During the course of the ceremonies the tomb is washed with rosewater and sandalwood paste, anointed with perfumes and covered with embroidered silk cloths, and for five nights henna paste is applied to the columns of the shrine, and *kalawa*, dyed thread, wrapped around the pillars supporting the canopy over the grave.

During the night a religious gathering assembles, with sacred readings and the distribution of sweetmeats. *Qawwals* (professional religious singers) chant spiritual songs on Sufism and the qualities of the Khwaja, and then comes a prayer for the eternal peace of the Saint's soul. About half-past one in the morning, the tomb is washed with rosewater and *qawwalis* are sung for another hour, during which tea is served; finally, at four in the morning, the service ends with more prayers and the presentation of bowls of squash and sandal paste to the congregation. While the *qawwalis* are sung, many spectators go into a shivering trance, crying aloud as they repeat phrases of the songs with the singers. This condition is known as *hal* (literally 'health'), and at times scores of such trances culminate in a highly emotional atmosphere. In 1963 it is said that some two thousand people stood up on their toes, remaining there for fifteen minutes, until the singers slowly eased their performance.

On the final day, about noon, musicians play joyously while fireworks and crackers are exploded. Ceremonial headgear is presented to the various holy men and a mourning service is held later in the day. During the course of the six days, one entire night is devoted to the reading of original sacred poems by their authors, including Hindu as well as Muslim poets from all parts of India.

64 Marble corridors, filled with resting pilgrims, leading to the Dargah of Muinuddin Chishti, Ajmer

CHAPTER SEVEN
Shrines of Rajasthan

There are said to be more than five thousand temples in Rajasthan, for wealthy Jain and Rajput princes have always been enthusiastic builders. Most Hindu or Jain temples have little internal space, for they were not intended for congregational worship; like sacred mountain caves, the dark, innermost sanctuary housing the image of the deity has only one entrance and no windows. It is the *garbha-griha*, the 'womb house', where the worshipper is reborn.

To reach this *garbha-griha* you first enter an open portico, the *ardha-mandapa*, where performances of sacred music and dance are given in honour of the divinity. Next comes a large columned hall, the *mandapa*, which in turn gives onto a vestibule attached to the *garbha-griha*, completing the tortuous journey to and from the womb.

The earliest Hindu temples were constructed of wood and clay, and have long since disappeared. So it is the Buddhist monuments that are the oldest surviving religious structures: those third-century BC remains at Bairat, between Alwar and Jaipur. The foundations of a large circular building, whose brick and wood superstructure has vanished, stand on a plateau terraced out of the rocky mountainside. This was the *chaitya* or hall of worship, originally with twenty-six octagonal pillars, an opening to the east and a circumambulatory passage. Among enormous fallen rocks on a higher plateau are the remains of a *vihara* or monastery where the great Mauryan emperor Ashoka is believed to have stayed – one of his many edicts is carved on a nearby rock.

Most of the Buddhist shrines contemporary with Bairat were carved from existing caves and, similarly, Jains made use of caves for their original shrines.

Like Hindu temples, most early Jain buildings were of perishable materials or, if of stone or brick, were destroyed by Muslim invaders who often used the materials to build mosques. There is an eighth-century Jain temple at Osian, following the classic Hindu pattern, and the *tirthankars* are portrayed in a stylized meditation position, each with his symbol of bull, conch-shell, lion or serpent. Pillars and ceilings are elaborately carved, often with Hindu deities, and heavenly musicians are portrayed elsewhere, while effigies of the donors are placed in passageways at the front or the rear.

Finally come the religious buildings of the Muslim conquerors, comparatively austere places of worship, with rare exceptions. The Rajputs bore the brunt of the Muslim invasions, and eventual alliances through marriage led to the newcomers spending a considerable amount of time at Ajmer, in the middle of the princely states. So it is there that you can see today one of the principal places of Muslim pilgrimage in India.

65 A partially submerged temple in the lake below the City Palace, Bundi, is dedicated to Varuna, the Aryan god of wind

With our ears may we hear what is good.
With our eyes may we behold thy righteousness.
Tranquil in body, may we who worship thee find rest.

Upanishads

Hindu craftsmen were employed to adapt temples, or to use old materials for new mosques. In this way, Islamic architecture was inevitably influenced by that of the Hindus and Jains. Originally each man would pray five times daily, wherever he happened to be. Gradually assembly-places were established where communal prayers were followed by a sermon; a simple walled enclosure with a pool for ablutions was made more practical by adding roofed verandas for shelter from sun and rain which, in colder climates, would be enclosed for warmth in winter. From these basic structures evolved the splendid mosques of marble, with their naves, the *mihrab* or prayer-niche facing Mecca and a *minbar* or pulpit. Perhaps unconsciously following the ancient idea of a link between earth and heaven, came the minaret from which the call to prayer would be made.

As you travel around Rajasthan you can see how all these theories have been put into practice. A few temples dedicated to the sun god, Surya, remain here and there, such as that at Osian, some 65 kilometres north of Jodhpur. Here in a lonely valley are located the remnants of some fifteen temples: the Sun Temple, typical of the Indo-Aryan style, stands on a raised plinth, representing the Vedic altar, and is dated to between the eighth and tenth centuries.

Details of this and other temples can be found in guide books, but look out for the Sun God himself, driving the *Saptaswa*, a seven-headed horse or maybe seven horses, drawing his chariot across the heavens, a concept believed to have sprung from Babylonian and Persian origins. You can see these especially well on the façade of the Sun Temple at Ranakpur where, to one side of the spectacular Jain temples, on a small wooded hill by a stream, stand two charming polygonal buildings. The older of the two looks remarkably like a Roman temple and was probably originally an open pavilion. Now the spaces between the columns have been blocked in with bricks. Next to it is a fourteenth-century white marble Surya temple covered with stylized carvings of Surya in his chariot.

Perhaps even more interesting is the remnant of an eighth-century Surya temple incorporated within the later Kalika Mata temple next to the palace of Princess Padmini in the fortress citadel of Chitor. Also erected on a massive plinth, this was originally a simple rectangular cella. Carvings of the Sun God and his chariot still remain on the wide walls; high above the dark entrance to the inner sanctuary, Surya is flanked by Shiva, Vishnu and Indra.

This intriguing shrine dedicated to Kalika, goddess of spiritual power, is approached through a gateway leading to a small courtyard dominated by an aged banyan tree. A brick platform surrounds the tree, supporting a number of small statues including lions, ancient symbols of the sun, and many tridents, all painted vermilion. The tridents are one of Shiva's symbols and Kali or Kalika, patron Goddess of Chitor, is one of the many forms of Shakti or Parvati, wife to Lord Shiva.

Worshippers in scarlet turbans sit before a bareheaded priest by a half-moon step up to the *garbha-griha*, whose entrance is usually concealed by a scarlet and gold curtain. When this is drawn back, Kalika is revealed wearing a crimson and silver robe, standing on an altar covered with a heavy scarlet cloth inset with mirrors. She was installed here when Maharana Hamir reconquered Chitor in the fourteenth century.

66 Silver sanctuary doors guard the temple of Jagat Pita Shri Brahma at Pushkar, one of the few Brahma temples in India. The milkmaid Gayatri stands next to the four-faced Brahma image (the fourth face cannot be seen from the front)

Like many Hindu temples, Jain places of worship also have sacred banyan or peepul trees growing within their precincts. One of the most unusual tree shrines is the Kalpa-vriksha mentioned in Chapter Five, crowning the Jain temple of Shri Chintamani Pashunath on the edge of the long-buried city of Lodurva. Rebuilt in the seventeenth century of the lovely pale golden limestone and marble of Jaisalmer, the temple is unique for the detailed reliefs of a royal couple, set in panels around the base of the *trigore*, a square, three-storeyed structure like a small ziggurat, with an open pavilion rising from the topmost section, out of which the tree 'grows'.

This temple is held in such veneration that normally visitors of other faiths are not allowed to enter nor to photograph it even from the exterior. A tunnel is said to run from the temple some sixteen kilometres to the present capital of Jaisalmer, where it surfaces in vaults beneath the fifteenth-century Sambhavnath Jain temple. Here, rare palm-leaf texts, astrological treatises and other ancient manuscripts are believed to have been stored after being brought from Lodurva when it was abandoned in the twelfth century.

Jaisalmer, with its magnificent *havelis* or mansions built by wealthy merchant princes, is also justly famed for its eight Jain temples in the walled hilltop fortress city. The Sambhavnath is one of the oldest and has a unique domed ceiling with exquisitely sculptured dancers accompanied by a solitary male musician. Attached to this small temple is the fifteenth-century Rishabdevji or Adinath, with more fine carvings including the *torana* or curved archway where, as in all Jain temples, visitors must leave any leather objects. Alluring carvings of lovers, dancers and musicians as well as of various Hindu deities adorn the pillars of the main hall, together with many *tirthankar* statues of all sizes, seated crosslegged in a circle, with jewelled 'third eyes' in their foreheads.

Possibly the best known of all Jain temples in Rajasthan are those of Ranakpur near Udaipur, and Dilwara on Mount Abu. Ranakpur, one of the five holy places of the Jains, is a small, lonely wooded glen among the Aravalli Hills, a place of great tranquillity and beauty populated by dancing peacocks and playful monkeys. The whitewashed wall enclosing the temple area is surmounted by two splendid golden lions, while equally magnificent caparisoned elephants are painted on either side of the archway. Just inside the entrance and too often missed by visitors, a small Shiva shrine stands on a carved stone platform. Surrounded by shade trees, a tiny Nandi bull kneels before an exquisite carving of Lord Shiva, and a small *lingam*.

The three fifteenth-century Jain temples are set in well-kept gardens with *dharamshalas* (simple accommodation for pilgrims) among the trees. Largest and most astonishing of the three is the Chaumukha or Trailokya Deepak, founded in 1449 by a Jain merchant, Dharanshah, with the encouragement and financial help of Rana Kumbha, the famed warrior, administrator and ruler of Mewar. The temple is somewhat overpowering in size, with an enormous basement covering 48,000 square feet (about 4,000 sq. m.), four subsidiary shrines, twenty-four pillared halls, eighty domes supported by four hundred columns, forty-four spires or *sikaras*, and five exceptionally large domes covering the sanctuaries. Altogether there are 1,444 intricately carved marble columns, no two exactly alike, and an immense peepul tree, reputed to be 350 years old, grows from one central courtyard, an example of

67 Mount Abu: shrine to Shiva, with a brass image of the Charan bard, Durasa Adha, and Nandi the bull

117

a living Kalpa-vriksha. Yet despite the vastness of the temple complex, the whole effect is one of light and grace.

Very early in Jain history the sect covered sacred mountain tops with shrines and sanctuaries that later developed into virtual temple cities. Abu, Rajasthan's only hill station, was originally a centre for the Shiva cult; it was not until the eleventh century that it became a renowned Jain stronghold. The Dilwara group of five Jain temples standing in an ancient mango grove is built of dazzling white marble from the Makrana quarries, and of these, two are quite exceptional, the Vimala Vasahi and the Neminath.

The Vimala Vasahi was built about 1021 by Vimal Shah, minister to the Raja Bhimdeo. One legend recounts how the minister was anxious to have a son, and also eager to build a magnificent temple. The Goddess Ambika, touched by his deep devotion, promised he could have one or the other but not both. Consulting his wife, Vimal decided on the temple, but had to pay an exceptionally heavy price for the land, giving the Brahmin owners sufficient gold coins to cover the entire area! Commemorating this generosity, a procession of stone elephants bearing statues of the founder and his family leads from a pavilion to the domed porch, while there is another statue of Vimal on horseback near the entrance. A roundel in the dome of the ceiling of the *mandapa* shows the Hindu goddess Saraswati enthroned with Loyana Sutradhara, the bearded architect, on her right, while a second architect, holding a measuring rod, is on her left.

Since the exterior of the building is quite plain, the incredibly lavish interior comes as all the more of a surprise. The art of the stone masons is unsurpassed in the elaborate screens, curved scroll arches and pillars as well as the stupendous domed ceiling with its flower pendant surrounded by dancing nymphs, giving an almost three-dimensional effect.

The Neminath or Luna Vasahi was built in 1231 by two brothers, Vastupala and Tejapala, both ministers to the ruler, and dedicated to the twenty-second *tirthankar*.

This too is a fantastic work of art, with a stalactite pendant hanging like a crystal chandelier from the central dome. The stone masons were said to have been offered rewards in silver equal to the weight of the marble filings, and in addition Tejapala offered the weight in gold of any further filings pared off after the work was completed. The result is a breathtaking lacy effect of unbelievable delicacy.

The great Mewar fortress of Chitor has no fewer than twenty-seven Jain temples, mainly built in the fifteenth century. A small twelfth-century Digambar temple stands by a seven-storey carved stone tower known as the Kirti Stambha, the Pillar of Fame, erected by a Jain merchant at the same time as the temple. Here is an example of the ancient columns that separated earth and sky, and this one undoubtedly served as a model for the later fifteenth-century Kumbha's Jai Stambha or Tower of Victory which is 37 metres high with nine storeys and stands near the Mahasati, site of the second *jauhar* of Chitor.

Another of these pillars of white marble, called the Man Stambha, Tower of Glory, stands in front of the Digambar Jain temple in Chandangaon village in the Sawai Madhopur district of Jaipur. Here the present temple of white marble was constructed on the red sandstone foundations of an older

68 A marble carving of the eleventh-century Paramara ruler of Mount Abu, Raja Jayamal, who killed three rampaging buffaloes with one arrow. The Paramaras claim descent from the Agnikula

building, still partially visible. The statue of the twenty-fourth *tirthankar*, Mahavira Swami, in the sanctuary was discovered by a cobbler, Kripa Das, who grazed his cows on the mound where the temple now stands. One cow began shedding her milk on the mound, and, digging here, the cobbler brought the statue to light and installed it in a makeshift shelter. Almost immediately devotees began visiting it. Today hundreds of pilgrims come to the village monthly, and every year a huge fair is held to commemorate the event. This is the only Jain temple where no restrictions are placed on worshippers, who include members of other religious communities, outnumbering the Jains almost three to one! Chamars – cobblers – regard the temple and its statue with particular devotion.

Another interesting Jain temple nearer Jaipur is in the village of Sanganer, where a Kirti Stambha or Pillar of Fame in white Makrana marble stands, not in front of the Digambar Jain temple but before a Hindu sanctuary dedicated to Krishna. All twenty-four of the *tirthankars* are installed in the Jain temple, where there is a small bas-relief of the original chief priest, by the inner portal, and painted dancers in Rajput dress, added after the initial construction. At least two enchanting little reliefs depict realistic camels and riders on one of the outer walls.

Two more Jain temples deserve mention before we pass on to the Hindu temples, and these were built by two brothers in Bikaner, in the fifteenth to sixteenth centuries. Both temples are in the Muslim quarter of the old city, and the larger of the two, the Bhandeshwar, stands on a high walled plinth with a Mughal-type domed pavilion over the main entrance. Carved wooden columns with dancing figures surround a dark sanctuary with gold chequered designs and a mass of reflecting mirrorwork. The outer circular *mandapa* features some fascinating secular frescoes around the inside of the dome, depicting battle scenes, local historical events and parades of elephants and camels, giving an unusual picture of Bikaner's past.

From the limestone sanctuary on the upper storey, so highly polished with shells that it appears to be of marble, one sees a complex of Hindu temples, including a charming Ganesha temple where the elephant-headed god wears a frivolous orange tutu, silver bands over his shoulders and a jaunty conical red and silver cap.

In a nearby garden is the smaller Neminath Sandeshwar Jain temple, with a gaudily painted interior dome. The brothers who built these two temples, Bhandeshwar and Sandeshwar, were merchants dealing in the luxury trade of *ghi* (clarified butter), around 1450. Neither brother had a son to carry on his name, and to compensate, each built a temple. Bhandeshwar, the older, was watching the foundations being laid when a fly fell into a container of *ghi*. He carefully removed the insect and put it on his shoe, as a good Jain should, to save the fly's life. But watchers misinterpreted his action as a sign of meanness, and thought that he could not afford to build the large structure he had planned. They tested him, saying that were the foundations to be covered entirely with the liquid butter the building would never collapse.

Bhandeshwar's unhesitating response was to empty all his containers of valuable *ghi* into the foundations, thus proving his sincerity.

69 A painted Jain temple at Sirohi, with a worshipper in the foreground

CHAPTER EIGHT
Temples & Mosques

Hindu temples are an extension of the idea of a personal deity, and are called 'Devalaya', the 'Home of the God'. Not only are they places of worship, but the centre of community activities, and since the god is also a landowner, his temple receives revenues from the land, local taxes and gifts from all classes of worshippers. In cases of need, the temple acts as a bank, lending money to needy members of the congregation. Village councils meet in its precincts and civil disputes are settled there. Often schools are attached to the Devalaya and scholars meet there in intellectual debates. Added to all this are the many officials, priests, accountants and so on, who find permanent employment in the temple.

Religious rites are known as *puja*, meaning 'worship', and it is believed that after special ceremonies over the image, the deity takes up his or her abode in it. *Puja* is an act of homage and also of entertainment, wherein the deity is treated as an honoured guest, offered water to wash the feet, flowers and sweetmeats or betel. In the morning the god is awakened with music, bells, and the blowing of conch-shells. After being bathed, dried and dressed in fresh robes, he or she is honoured with incense: lamps are swung before the altar while garlands are placed around the neck. Rice and fruit are offered and the deity is believed to take an invisible share, leaving the material food for the worshippers. In the larger temples, dancing-girls and musicians entertain the deity; on festival days, the image is carried around the city in a chariot, sometimes pulled by the devotees heading a great procession.

Communal worship as such is not usual, although large numbers of people, an audience rather than a congregation, do watch many of the *puja* services; generally, worshippers attend the temple in small family groups, or alone, to make private acts of homage.

The buildings themselves range from the ornate and wealthy to the very simplest, such as the little Vishvakarma in Bikaner, one of the few devoted to Brahma, opposite the elaborate Bhandeshwar Jain temple. The Vishva-karma is mainly patronized by carpenters, and its otherwise plain façade is adorned with a charming and amusing frieze of dancing figures and musicians as well as craftsmen, such as carpenters, glass-blowers and silver-smiths, all painted in white silhouettes on a terracotta ground. Inside the sanctuary, with its image of Brahma wearing an orange robe, gold necklace and crown, the *garbha-griha* doorway is flanked by intricately carved old wooden panels protected by glass and donated by the carpenters who founded the temple.

70 The carved columns and ceiling of the *mandapa* in the Neminath temple, one of the Dilwara group of Jain temples at Mount Abu

With a multitude of Hindu temples hidden in jungles, palaces, cities and villages, it is difficult to select just a few. There are many varied and charming examples: temples mysteriously half-submerged in lakes, such as those in Alwar, Nagda and Bundi; the ninth- and tenth-century temples of Harihara and Harisagiri at Osian, with their exquisite carvings; the temple of Charbhujinath in the quaint twisting lanes of the walled town of the same name, between Ranakpur and Nathdwara, with its startling Black Vishnu statue within a silver-framed sanctuary.

In Sanderao, a village between Jodhpur and Ranakpur, the Shiva temple of Nimeshuwar Mahadeo is hidden within a high enclosure. In the outer courtyard stand two enormous black elephant statues caparisoned in scarlet and yellow and carrying riders, possibly donors of the temple. On the same platform are several pavilions, and shade trees from whose lower branches hang large bells struck by passing devotees. A two-storey, colonnaded portal leads to an inner enclosure with a black and white marble courtyard; there, wide steps mount to a higher platform, on which stands the main Shiva temple. Eight or nine figures of Nandi the bull recline before it, ranging from charming little brass bulls like puppies to almost life-sized ones in marble, adorned with fresh marigolds and silver saddlecloths.

Participating in services such as these even in less attractive surroundings is always an emotional experience. The Govind Devji in Jaipur, the rulers' own temple dedicated to Lord Krishna, is not particularly distinguished for its architecture. It consists of an open columned pavilion with a slightly sunken courtyard, enclosed by a low marble balustrade. The image of Govind Deva, the most sacred of the six forms of Krishna and the tutelary divinity of the ruler, was sculpted by Vajranath, an unrivalled sculptor of his age and the great-grandson of Krishna himself. It is concealed behind three curtains, one in front of the other, and directly faces the bedroom of the Maharaja of Jaipur in the old City Palace, at the other end of the extensive Jai Vilas gardens.

On special occasions the ruler would stand at his window worshipping the image from afar; the Maharajas styled themselves 'Govind-Diwan' (ministers of Govind, who was regarded as the real ruler of Jaipur). The deity is shown with the typical dark blue countenance of Krishna, playing a flute and wearing a heavy crown with elaborate robes and garlands. His consort Radha sits beside him. Vajranath is said to have made three different statues of Krishna incarnations, showing each in turn to his grandmother whose father was Lord Krishna himself, and asking each time if he had made a true portrait. Each of the first two images had some fault, but with the third his grandmother was completely satisfied. The first two statues are also housed in temples in Jaipur, and devout pilgrims who come from the other side of India will visit all three divinities in one day.

Anyone, including foreign tourists, may witness the *darshan* or 'viewing' daily, many sitting under the trees listening to holy men expounding the scriptures. At 11.15 am, the priests appear and ceremoniously draw back each of the three gold and silver curtains in turn, swinging small lamps as they do so. The *darshan* is an ecstatic occasion as the crowds stare in silence at the sacred image, then raise their arms and in a great collective sigh, call out, 'We hunger to see your face and we wish to have you constantly in our

71 The Govind Devji temple at Jaipur: a priest reciting from the sacred scriptures while worshippers wait for the temple doors to be opened, when they will see the images of Radha and Krishna

thoughts and to meditate on your lotus feet. This life is full of responsibilities and now we are in the middle of the ocean; please give us your blessing so that we can relieve ourselves of life's burdens and understand the meaning of life.'

As the curtains fall to conceal the deity once more, the crowds file from left to right, around the back of the shrine and out again into the courtyard where priests give each a small *prasad* ('Gift of God'), a piece of fruit or sweetmeat, that they have blessed. The ceremony takes place five or seven times daily, and each time the costume of the deity is changed. Food is served twice, rice and fruit at 11.30 am, and fried food at 7 pm, distributed by the *pujaris* to the congregation who give, in exchange, coupons bought earlier. Some of the food is eaten by the purchasers themselves, who distribute the remainder to those who cannot afford the coupons.

In Kota, drums and flutes played in a gallery over the entrance to the Matharadeesh Krishna temple near the Patan Pol gate announce prayers and the unveiling of the deity. The temple houses the First Lord of the important Vallabacharya sect. And some six or seven kilometres outside Kota city is a little-known but utterly charming group of eighth-century temples clustered around a small lake, among groves of shade trees – a secret place this, enclosed within high stone walls; small figures of Nandi and finely carved *trimurthi* and *chaumurthi* heads (three- and four-faced statues) are scattered in the courtyards; bathing ghats and eighteenth-century pavilions are peopled by hermits and pilgrims. The main shrine, dedicated to Mahadevi Shiva, was reconstructed by the Mauryan ruler Shergan in 738 and was again renovated in 1751.

Peacocks are the outstanding memories of the Gulab Dasji ki Baghichi Mandir at Sikar, a couple of hours' drive from Jaipur. In the outer courtyard a baby peacock occupies a basket, watched over by a calf; the entrance to the inner courtyard, set between columned verandas, features a pair of gay peacocks painted over the carved doorways. A large peepul tree grows in the smaller, inner court where pilgrims from distant Bengal and elsewhere cook and serve meals to local women as part of their offering to the shrine.

This is a combination of temple and ashram and attracts barren women who offer coconuts in the hope of conception. Other supplicants suffer from a skin disease caused by wearing the lac bangles so popular in Rajasthan. After praying, they hang the bangles before the shrine entrance, together with coconuts and bunches of hair cut from one-year-old boys in the *mandan* hair-cutting ceremony. Once a year, on the night of the Sacred New Moon, all the hair is collected and thrown into a nearby spring, during a local, six-day *mela*.

A few kilometres outside Sikar rises the steep hill of Harshanath. It takes about half an hour to drive the fifteen kilometres of snaking road up the fifteen-hundred-metre-high hill, passing pilgrims plodding on foot. The effort is well worth while. At the summit, with glorious views across the plain, stands a complex of ruined temples built by the Chauhan Rajputs a thousand years ago. Here the tumbled stones of the ancient temples have been roughly reassembled to form small shrines with some of the most delicate carvings imaginable, often replaced upside down in walls and ceilings. Vishnu, surrounded by dancers and musicians; Shiva performing his Tandava dance; the Tree of Life, Surya symbols, peacocks, the Pandava brothers – a glorious mixture of themes is depicted here, but the finest carvings are now in a small museum in Sikar itself, often, alas, closed.

Vermilion-painted figures with pink satin skirts and fresh garlands denote the respect these ancient shrines still command. One group is especially intriguing: three crude figures fashioned from one piece of stone represent Durgadevi flanked by the Black and White Bhairons. All three are coloured brilliant vermilion with blank eyes, eyebrows and noses picked out in gold, and slivers of coloured paper pasted over the images which are adorned with garlands of marigolds and jasmine.

Not to be missed is a temple to Brahma, the Jagat Pita Shri Brahma Mandir at Pushkar. Standing high on a plinth approached by steep marble steps, it has an unusual marble floor inset with hundreds of silver rupees together with the names of their donors, surrounding a silver turtle, a *kacchawa*, facing the *garbha-griha*. This was presented by a pilgrim in 1947 and the coins, which are also embedded in the walls of the cloisters, include many British ones from the Victorian period; they commemorate the births and deaths of loved ones.

Peacocks strut along the temple walls, appropriately enough since they are the vehicle of Brahma's consort, Saraswati, although it is the tiny image of her rival, the milkmaid Gayatri, that flanks that of the Chaumurthi, the four-faced, black image of Brahma. A young bearded priest in long white cotton robe over a cream, ankle-length gown attends the shrine, which is guarded by a finely carved marble gateway before the silver sanctuary doors. Steps in a corner of the cloisters lead to a small cave in the rocky foundations, made into a temple to Lord Shiva.

Finally come two of the most unusual and fascinating Hindu temples, those of Ram Deora and the Deshnoke Rat Temple.

Ram Deora was born in 1458, a Rajput of the Tomar clan, and a descendant of the famed twelfth-century hero, Prithviraj Chauhan. Ram Deoji is said to have miraculously appeared as a babe in a cradle by the side of the newborn son of a hitherto childless couple, and he grew to be an invincible hero, devoting his life to the poor. He is worshipped by Hindus of all castes, especially by untouchables. Muslims also revere him, calling him Ram Shah Pir, following the visit of five Muslim holy men from Mecca. During a period of testing, Ram Deoji miraculously produced eating utensils the holy men had left behind in Mecca, and this convinced them of his saintliness.

Eventually Ram Deoji buried himself alive, and contrary to traditional Hindu custom which demands that corpses shall be cremated, his followers bury their dead.

The temple is approached through a massive red sandstone gateway from the lofty portal of which is suspended a bell for pilgrims to sound. Women whose arms are literally hidden beneath scores of ivory bangles clasp children as they walk between whitewashed walls past Muslim graves and ash-covered *sadhus*. One platform supports several small *chhatris* with carvings of heroes on horseback and many charming toy horses, while in a covered pavilion orange-turbaned musicians play enthusiastically on enormous drums. Carved wooden doors portraying Ram Deoji with

typically Rajput curled beard and moustache lead into the main shrine, a dark room with a platform on which rest life-sized model horses donated by worshippers, including one of silver, complete with panoply and riders.

A silver bust of Ram Deoji wearing a crown, with a shocking-pink silk cloth around the neck and a garland of jasmine and marigolds, surmounts a low table before a grille enclosing three small graves. The original head priest and his family are buried here, their graves covered with a pink silk cloth, and the chief priest of the shrine is always the eldest son of the direct descendant of Ram Deoji. Opposite the shrine is a smaller one where his adopted daughter, Dallibhai, is buried, and this is also flanked by model horses.

The significance of the horses stems from the fact that, as a true Rajput, Ram Deoji was greatly attached to his horse and together they covered immense distances, rendering help to those in distress and conquering many enemies. Even a wooden replica of the horse miraculously transported grain to drought-stricken areas.

Among all Rajasthan's temples, the Karni Mata between Bikaner and Jodhpur must be unique, for its most important occupants are legions of small brown rats. The temple is dedicated to an early-fifteenth-century female saint who was a mystic reincarnation of Durga, the goddess of power, and was born in 1387 near Phalodi. As the sixth daughter, she was a great disappointment to the family hoping for a son. Her father's sister went so far as to curse the baby, while patting her on the head – when all five of her fingers stuck together. Before her birth, the child's mother had dreamed that the Goddess Durga was to be reincarnated as the baby girl, and belatedly remembering this the aunt named the child Karanji, 'one who will achieve something'. Years later, while bathing the child using only her one good hand, the aunt found her damaged fingers suddenly recovered.

After performing miracles and foretelling the future early in her life, Karanji dedicated herself to the service of the poor. She is said to have laid the foundations of the fortress of Jodhpur in 1458, prophesying that the dynasty would rule until the 'twenty-eighth step', and when Prince Bika, son of the Jodhpur ruler, was on his way to found his own kingdom of Bikaner in 1465, he visited Karanji for her blessing.

Karanji was 151 years old when she visited her sisters, in whose village lived a blind carpenter, Bana. Karanji offered to restore his sight temporarily just so that he could see her and carve her image; when it was finished she told him to put the carving under his head when he went to bed. He would wake up to find himself at Deshnoke where he was to place the image in a cave and his eyesight would then be restored permanently.

Today she is known as Karni Mati. On important occasions her image is dressed in clothes from the royal Bikaner house, whose rulers never engaged in battle without first seeking the saint's blessing. Silver pendants depicting Karni Mati are on sale at stalls outside the temple, and on the silver doors of the sanctuary she is shown with the sun and the moon and a pair of rats on either side. The rats come into the story in this way.

Being a Charan by birth, from a family of traditional bards, Karni Mati was once brought the body of an only son who had just died, the parents begging her to restore him to life or else their line would die out. In a deep

72 The Karni Mata temple at Deshnoke: a priest feeding the rats

trance Karni confronted Yama, the God of Death, asking for the boy's soul, but Yama told her that this was no longer in his power to grant as it had already been reincarnated. Karni swore then that none of the Charans should ever come under Yama's powers but that when they died they should inhabit the bodies of rats, and when the rats died they would resume life as Charans once again.

One might suppose that walking barefoot on the marble floor before the sanctuary or around it, where the entire area is a mass of moving rats, would be utterly repellent. But in fact the little creatures are intent on their own business, scurrying to eat the quantities of rice in the area immediately before the altar, tended by a turbaned priest. Dozens of rats gather around a metal bowl of sweetened milk, tails forming a lacy fringe as their heads dip into the dish. The unwary visitor who happens to injure or kill one has to make reparation by donating a gold or silver rat. The live rats are called *kabas* and are said to be a unique species; during a local plague transmitted by rats, in 1927, nobody in the vicinity of the temple caught the disease.

Muslim shrines, although comparatively few, also hold an important place in Rajasthan. The tomb of the Sufi saint Khwaja Shah Hamiduddin, who died over seven hundred years ago in Nagaur, not far from Deshnoke, is not unlike many Hindu shrines with its high entrance gateway, kitchens for pilgrims and the tomb itself standing in the shade of a grove of trees.

The mosque in the tiny Muslim state of Tonk is of special interest because of its bold mixture of secular Mughal and austere Islamic styles of architecture. Dominating the small capital are the four high *minars* of the mosque, with its arched colonnades where classes are held in the shade. The façade of the building is elaborately painted to resemble inlaid marble, while the interior is more like a palace throne-room than the usually plain Muslim place of worship.

Most famed of Muslim shrines is that of the Sufi saint Muinuddin Chishti at Ajmer, which Muslims call Ajmer Sharif – Holy Ajmer.

Khwaja Chishti was a Persian born in Seistan in 1142, a direct descendant of Ali, son-in-law of the Prophet. He grew up in Khurasan where he witnessed the terrible massacres of Central Asian invaders, and decided to renounce the world, selling his ancestral home and joining a renowned mystic, Khwaja Usman Haruni. Haruni was a Caliph belonging to the Sufi school of the Chishtia order, Chisht being a village in Khurasan and one of the four seats of Sufism adhering strictly to Koranic law. The word 'Sufi' is taken from *suf* (wool), from which is made the heavy garment worn by Sufis as a mark of penitence.

For twenty years Chishti stayed with Haruni who finally appointed him Caliph, ordaining him as a missionary when he left for India in 1186. In a dream he had been instructed to carry out his mission in Ajmer and he arrived in that city during the reign of the famed Rajput warrior-diplomat, Prithviraj, then engaged in battles with Sultan Ghori and his armies who were invading India from Afghanistan. In fact, Chishti remained in Ajmer for the rest of his life, during which the city was captured by the Afghans; the Sufi missionary, however, calmly established a code of moral, social and intellectual conduct among his disciples and in 1256, at the age of 114, Muinuddin Chishti entered his cell for prayers for the last time. He had told

73 Tarkashin's or Atarkin's gateway at Nagaur, built in the early fourteenth century. The Sufi shrine of Sheikh Hamiduddin Nagauri lies beyond

his followers not to disturb him and they obeyed this injunction for six days. When they finally opened the cell door, they found the saint was dead, and it is in commemoration of those six days that the Urs is held for the same period annually.

Chishti's powers remained long after his death. More than three centuries later the Mughal emperor Akbar, who had no son despite his many wives, made the pilgrimage barefoot from Agra to the saint's tomb to pray for an heir. It was a member of the Sufi Chishti order, Salim Chishti, living at Sikri, who actually prophesied that the emperor would have three sons, and when in 1569 the first of these was born, he was named Salim after the Sikri prophet. Later Akbar built his city of Fatehpur Sikri on the red sandstone hill where the hermit had his cave. (Salim was to become the Emperor Jahangir.) Khwaja Chishti of Ajmer was honoured with a mosque which Akbar built by his tomb, and for his frequent journeys to Ajmer the emperor also built himself a palace in that city.

The saint's tomb is in the centre of the bazaar area of the old city and is approached through a high gateway with splendid silver doors; a second courtyard is entered through another great gate, the Boland Darwaza.

A number of buildings are housed within the enclosure, including an elegant mosque built by Shah Jahan, with a long inscription in Persian, and a smaller mosque constructed by Jahangir.

Opposite the main entrance to the tomb itself is a colonnaded veranda with black and white marble paving where many pilgrims, including Sikhs and Hindus, rest while awaiting the distribution of food. Among the trees in the courtyard are several more graves, including that of the saint's own daughter, Bibi Hafiz Jamal, and one of Emperor Shah Jahan's daughters, Chimni Begum, as well as that of a humble water-carrier who saved the Emperor Humayun's life by ferrying the defeated king across a river after his battle with Sher Shah Suri.

Inside the shrine itself devotees move slowly around the heavy silver double rails guarding the tomb with its gold-embroidered canopy, the crowds jostling to kiss the grille enclosing it.

The other important Muslim edifice in Ajmer is the Arhai (or Adhai)-din-ka Jhonpra, the 'Two-and-a-half-day Shelter', which Tod, enthusing over the 'gorgeous prodigality of ornament', wrote could vie with the noblest buildings in the world. This great mosque was originally a Jain religious college within a temple. Built in 1153, it was damaged by Muhammad Ghori when he seized Ajmer. At that time, Ghori took the remains of many surrounding temples, together with the ruined college (some estimate that parts of at least thirty temples were used), to build the mosque, which tradition alleges was miraculously completed in two and a half days.

Probably about 1200 Qutbuddin added a massive pierced stone screen of seven arches, exquisitely fashioned, in front of the original pillared hall where no two of the intricately carved columns are alike. Now in ruins, the mosque was originally even larger than the famous Qutb near Delhi, and has ten domes in a roof upheld by a hundred and twenty-four columns. Two delicate, broken minarets with Kufic and Tughra inscriptions from the Koran stand on the corners above the central high arch of the screen.

*If any worshipper do reverence with
    faith to any god whatever,
I make his faith firm,
    and in that faith he reverences
    his god,
And gains his desires,
    for it is I who bestow them.*
                                    Bhagavad Gita

74 A silver tortoise (kacchawa), donated by a worshipper, is embedded in the floor of the Brahma temple at Pushkar. Offerings of flowers are scattered on the tortoise

III
SUN, MOON &
FIRE

In a Rajput I always recognize a friend.
Colonel James Tod

A man should first choose his king,
then his wife.
And only then amass wealth.
For without a king in the world,
where would wife and property be?
Mahabharata

CHAPTER NINE
Sons of Kings

Kingship may at first seem irrelevant in writing of Rajasthan today, but in fact the concept colours every aspect of life in the area.

Until comparatively recently this was truly 'The Land of Kings'. The power and privileges of the princes had been severely curtailed since Partition in 1947 but for some, such as the late Maharaja of Jaipur, who in 1949 was appointed the first Rajpramukh or Head of State of the newly-formed Greater Rajasthan Union, a titular status still remained. Eight of the nineteen maharajas of former Rajput states attended his inauguration in Jaipur, which was to be the capital of the new union. The Maharao Raja of Kota was appointed Deputy Rajpramukh and the Maharana of Udaipur, as the most senior of all the Rajput princes, was given the title of Maharajpramukh and was to take precedence on all formal occasions.

Now even the nominal courtesies have gone, but a Government edict cannot wipe out centuries of tradition and the mystic charisma of the princes. They may now be known officially as Shri and Shrimati – Mr and Mrs – but to the people who have always regarded them as their *man-bap* (father and mother) the traditional respect remains and they are still 'Your Highness', to be greeted with folded palms and the token touching of the feet.

The very name Rajput is a corruption of Raja-Putra, meaning Sons of Kings, and Singh, a surname given to many Rajputs, signifies 'lion', a creature with the essentially kingly qualities of invincibility and courage. The title Raja comes from Ranjayatri ('He who Pleases'), while court bards describe the king as 'father of his people' and 'the husband of his realm'.

The princes of the desert kingdom of Jaisalmer have as one of their hereditary titles 'The Lord of Yadava', protected by the divine umbrella which was given to Krishna by Yadava. And because silver is the colour of the moon and favoured by Krishna, the royal howdah of Jaisalmir in which the rulers ride on their state elephants is of silver rather than the more usual gold. Moreover, the palace contains nearly eight hundred items of silver furniture. When the ruler is away, his throne, on which even his children are not allowed to sit, is occupied by a portrait of Lord Krishna, known to the family affectionately as 'Little Brother'.

The Rathores of Bikaner and Marwar and the Sisodias of Mewar, on the other hand, are among the Suryavansh, clans claiming descent from Rama, an incarnation of the sun. (Tod has a theory linking the ancestors of Mewar with the last of the Persian Sassanians.) Regarded as the senior of the three groups are the Agnikula, 'fireborn', superior because they were created not of woman but from the sacred firepit on holy Mount Abu. Among these are

75 A painting of the nineteenth-century Maharana Sajjan Singhji, in Udaipur City Palace, shows the ruler draped in jewels and with a white Shiva symbol painted between the eyes

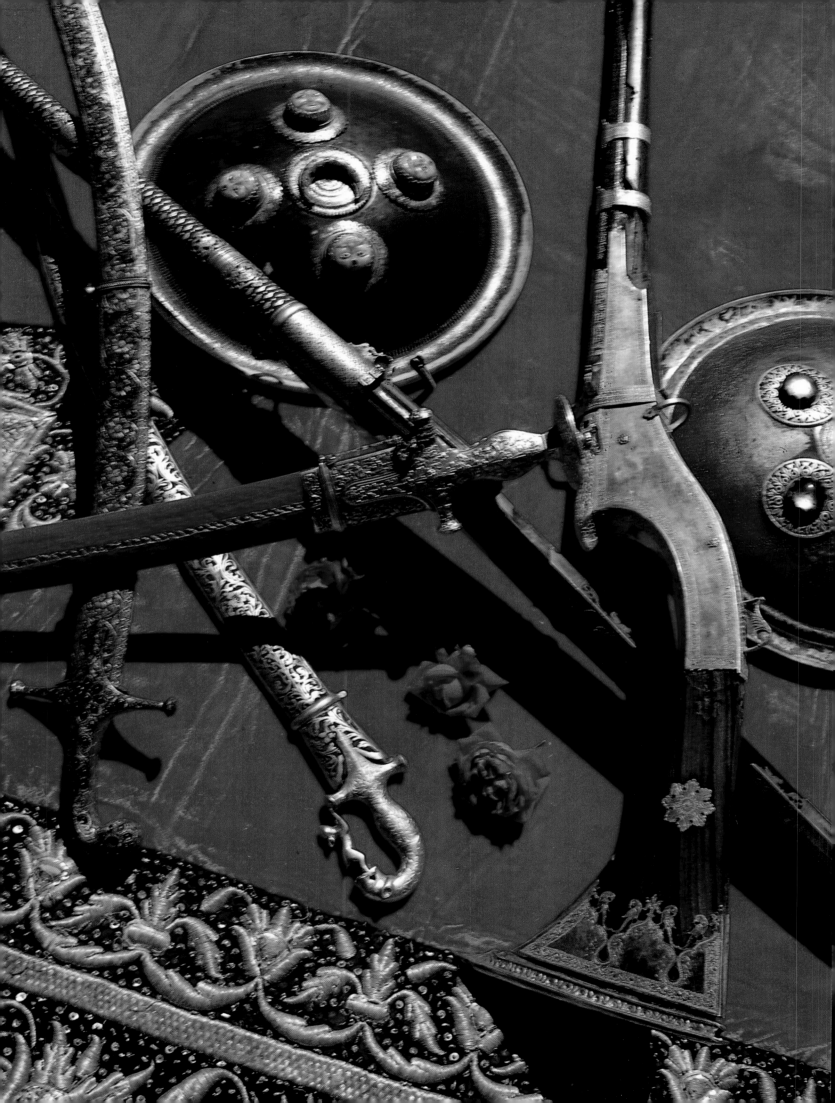

the Hara Chauhans of Bundi and Kota, the Chauhans of Delhi and Ajmer, and the Deoras of Sirohi.

The mystic powers with which the king was endowed at his consecration were strengthened during his reign by such ancient ceremonies as the Asvamedha, the royal horse sacrifice, which ensured the future fertility and growth of the kingdom. Such a ceremony, not to be undertaken lightly for it might end in disastrous wars, would, if successful, confirm the status of the ruler as a semi-divine emperor and had been practised by the Gatae tribes in Persia long before the Christian era, and certainly by the Scythians who were to invade India.

A specially consecrated milk-white stallion dedicated to the sun would be liberated to wander at will for a year. A select band of warriors would follow the horse, and the chieftains or kings on whose territory it roamed had either to do homage to the sacrificer, forfeiting their sovereignty, or go to war. If the horse was not captured by a neighbouring ruler, implying defiance, it was brought back to the capital at the end of the year, by which time its royal owner had annexed more territory.

Throughout the year the ruler would undergo intensive purification rites combined with penances and asceticism. Meanwhile a special sacrificial enclosure would be constructed of twenty-one octagonal wooden pillars, covered with golden plates, and magnificent materials and garlands. All the neighbouring princes would be summoned to the ceremony and after the stallion was ritually suffocated, there followed a macabre symbolic ceremony by the chief queen.

The maharani would lie down as though mating with the dead horse, while the maharaja would recite a long invocation including a petition to the stallion to 'lay thy seed well in the channel of the one who has opened her thighs ...' Hundreds of Brahmin priests took part in the ceremony, dismembering the dead horse and removing the marrow to be cooked and offered to the ruler. In this way he ate the 'spirit' of the sacred horse on behalf of his people, just as the queen had symbolically been absorbed into the masculine strength of the animal. In addition, hundreds of small animals and birds were sacrificed, cooked and their flesh distributed to the gathering.

Whether descendants of sun, moon or fire, all the royal families can relate dramatic tales of their forebears. Nearly every great fortified city in Rajasthan bears witness to the Rajput's obsession with honour. Death in its most violent form was to be preferred to the shame of capitulation, so that when defeat in battle seemed inevitable men and women would embrace certain death, dressed in their wedding finery. Such a mass suicide was known as *jauhar*.

Most famed of all are the three devastating sieges of Udaipur's early capital of Chitor, when thousands of Rajput men, women and children, led by their rulers, deprived their attackers of the fruits of victory.

The thirteen kilometres of battlements towering on the flat summit of Chitor, some 152 metres above the plain, enclose not only many palaces and fortresses but temples, colleges, bazaars, granaries – in fact, an entire city. In addition, today there is a small park of wild game as well. But above all it has water, reservoirs and lakes that can support thousands of inhabitants.

Traditionally it was Prince Bhim, one of the Pandava heroes of the

76 A collection of ceremonial swords, shields and guns from the Royal Armoury of the maharaja of Jodhpur

Mahabharata, who, hoping to learn the secret of immortality, became a disciple of a wise man living on the summit of the cliff. However, the impatient prince omitted some of the essential rites and in his frustration stamped so angrily and with such force that he created an enormous hole from which gushed a spring of clear water. Today a large reservoir bears the name of Bhimlat Kund, with terraces of shallow steps to the water level. The ruins of the Bundi prince's palace, as well as the *chhatris* of many queens, not to mention numerous temples including the Adbhutnath with its splendid three-faced Shiva in black marble, emerge from the surrounding wilderness.

Padmini's palace, a charming water-pavilion (today a replica of the thirteenth/fourteenth-century original), was the setting for Chitor's first siege in 1303. Padmini was an exceptionally beautiful princess from Sri Lanka, married to the Chitor chieftain, Rawal Ratan Singh. Although she observed strict purdah, the fame of her beauty had spread throughout India, and reached the ears of the Sultan of Delhi, Alauddin Khilji. Anxious to annex the wealthy Rajput states, the Sultan had been encamped below Chitor's ramparts for many months, and the siege was beginning to have serious effects on the defenders when the Sultan sent them an astonishing message. He would raise the siege in exchange for the beauteous Padmini.

The offer was indignantly refused, but eventually the Sultan suggested a compromise, agreeing to withdraw his forces if he could only see the princess's reflection in a mirror, thus preserving her honour.

The Rajputs realized this was most probably an excuse for Alauddin to study the inner defences of the fortress, but they agreed to lead the Sultan through the great gates to a secluded palace on the banks of the lake, where the queen and her ladies spent the cool evenings. Alauddin was taken to a room overlooking the lake and the water-pavilion, as are visitors today. Then, as now, a mirror on the wall opposite the window reflected the steps from the pavilion to the water's edge. For a few seconds as he sat with his back to the window, facing the mirror, the Emperor of Delhi was able to glimpse the graceful figure of the woman whose legendary beauty had brought him to this humiliating situation.

But the shimmering reflection of the exquisite Rani had more than justified the rumours, and when, having fulfilled his part of the bargain, her husband courteously escorted the Sultan through the gates to the very foot of the cliff, Rawal Ratan suddenly found himself made a prisoner.

The ruler's followers were informed that the price of his release and of the Sultan's withdrawal from Chitor would be the complete surrender of Padmini. The Maharani accepted the conditions but insisted that, as befitted both the Sultan's rank and her own, she should be escorted by her ladies and retinue. And so seven hundred palanquins, each screened with purdah curtains and carried by six bearers, accompanied Padmini's royal palanquin. In the seclusion of the Muslim camp, husband and wife were allowed half an hour's farewell. As Alauddin grew restless, the curtains of the palanquins were suddenly drawn, revealing the fully-armed pick of Rajput nobility, instead of the expected womenfolk. In spite of this surprise they were still too few to reach the well-guarded emperor, although their desperate hand-to-hand battles did enable Padmini and her husband to reach the gates of Chitor in safety.

77 Portrait of Maharaja Taqat Singh of Jodhpur, behind the throne with its ceremonial flywhisks, symbols of state, in the Umaid Bhavan Palace, Jodhpur

Many Rajputs lost their lives on that occasion, but Alauddin also lost so many of his own troops that he was forced to retire for the time being. Soon, however, he returned with reinforcements. Weakened by the loss of so many of their own forces, the Rajputs again faced certain defeat, and one night Rawal Ratan had a vision in which Kalika, patron goddess of the fort, announced that she was not content with the eight thousand kinsmen who had already been killed, but that she must have royal victims, and that each of the ruler's twelve sons must be crowned and mount the *gadi* in turn, reigning for three days. On the fourth day the new ruler should meet the enemy and death and another brother be enthroned in his stead. 'Unless the twelve who wore the diadem' gave their lives, the Mewars would lose Chitor for ever.

The princes competed for the honour of being the first to die, but Rawal Ratan determined to save his second and favourite son, Ajaisi. When eleven of his sons had been crowned in so macabre a fashion, the ruler insisted on Ajaisi's escaping through the enemy lines to continue the dynasty. Once he was safely away, Ratan himself became the twelfth king to be sacrificed. Now the final act of *jauhar* was inevitable. Padmini, with the other queens, princesses and wives and daughters of the garrison, put on their bridal gowns and all their jewellery and walked through the underground tunnels whose entrance can be seen today by the massive Rana Kumbha's palace.

Padmini brought up the rear and the entrance was blocked behind her. Thirteen thousand singing women threw themselves into a vast funeral pyre, and afterwards their menfolk smeared their foreheads with the ashes and dressed in their own saffron wedding robes. In a final frenzy, they sallied out to fight to the death and 'went laughing to heaven'.

Alauddin's triumph was an empty one. When the conqueror marched through the gateways he entered a dead city, still stinking of the burnt flesh of Padmini and her loyal followers. Furious, he destroyed temples and palaces with the sole exception of the one from which he had glimpsed Padmini, and her water-pavilion. (Some two and a half centuries later, at the third sack of Chitor, the Mughal emperor Akbar took the golden gates of Padmini's pavilion and set them up in his fort at Agra.)

Ten years after Alauddin's capture of Chitor, it was retaken by Hamir Singh of the younger branch of the family. The rulers' title was not 'Raja' but 'Rana', and all future rulers of Mewar were known as Maharana.

Hamir became the paramount Hindu ruler of Northern India, to whom the other Rajput princes paid homage. His grandson Lakha restored many of the buildings on Chitor, besides constructing dams, reservoirs and lakes, all subsidized by the recently developed silver and zinc mines at Zawar.

There followed several generations of powerful Mewar rulers, notably Maharana Sanga who won eighteen pitched battles against Ibrahim Lodi, king of Delhi, and another against the forces of the Emperor Babur himself. Despite losing an eye and a hand and suffering eighty-four wounds on his body, Sanga did not die on the battlefield but was probably poisoned in 1527. Since his two elder sons were dead, his third, Ratan Singh, inherited Chitor and married, among other princesses, Karnavati, sister of the Bundi ruler. Ratan died only five years later and Karnavati, who was bearing his child, did not join him on his pyre. Instead (as related in Chapter Four) she claimed the protection of the Emperor Humayun as 'brother' when, during the second

78 One of the young princes of the Jodhpur royal family on horseback. The inward-pointing ears are typical of the Jodhpur breed of horses

siege of Chitor in 1533 by Sultan Bahadur Shah of Gujarat, she smuggled her baby son Udai Singh to safety. Her real brother, with five hundred kinsmen, was killed when a section of the ramparts was mined by the attacking Sultan's Portuguese sappers.

With no time to prepare a sufficiently huge funeral pyre, Karnavati led thousands of women and children, clad in bridal gowns and jewellery, to underground magazines and storerooms full of gunpowder and combustibles, and they were blown to eternity. The remaining warriors, carrying the *changi*, the Mewar royal insignia of a golden sun on black peacock-feathers, charged to their final mortal combat with the attackers.

Altogether thirty-two thousand Rajput warriors lost their lives in the second sack of Chitor; every clan lost its chief, but Rana Vikramaditya, who had succeeded his dead brother Ratan, managed to cut his way through the battlefield to safety.

Humayun had hastened to the rescue but, having to march across the whole of India from Bengal, arrived too late to save Karnavati and Chitor; he did, though, eventually restore the city to Vikramaditya, who promised to protect the infant prince, Udai. Vikramaditya, however, proved an arrogant and unpopular ruler and was assassinated by Banbir, a distant kinsman, who was made Regent. Udai Singh was about six years old when Banbir decided to get rid of the child and assume full ruling powers. The boy was asleep when Panna, his nurse, heard screams from the ladies' palace where Banbir had already begun searching for the little prince.

Quickly the nurse put the boy into a fruit basket, covering him with leaves, and giving it to a manservant to carry to safety, she substituted her own son in the prince's cradle. Banbir plunged his sword into the boy and the body, which everyone assumed was that of the prince, was immediately consumed on a funeral pyre. The loyal Panna joined the prince and the manservant and together they searched in vain for refuge until the Bhils, original rulers of Mewar, came to the rescue, taking the exhausted trio to the massive, impregnable fortress of Kumbhalgarh, deep in the forested ravines of the Aravallis.

Here, Udai grew up as the 'nephew' of the Jain Governor, but gradually the Mewar nobles recognized the lad as their rightful ruler. Before he was thirteen he was invested as the Maharana of Chitor, and Banbir was deposed.

Unfortunately Udai was not cast in the heroic mould of his ancestors. A new Mughal emperor, Babur's grandson Akbar, greatest of them all, was to attack Chitor in 1567/8 and the fortress city never recovered from this third siege. Unlike his predecessors, Udai was not prepared to sacrifice his own life. Instead he fled, leaving the defence to his loyal vassals. Two young chieftains, Jaimal of Badnor and Patta of Kelwa, neither more than sixteen years old, were the heroes of this final sack. Patta had recently been married – his father had died in an earlier battle – and his mother not only commanded him to 'put on the saffron robe' but armed herself and her young daughter-in-law with lances, and all three rode down the steep cliff path to die together in their hopeless attack on Akbar's trained forces.

This was really the end of Chitor. Once again the *jauhar* was ordered. Nine queens, five princesses and their babies and the families of all the nobles still living in Chitor died on the funeral pyre. Tod records that thirty

79 The Rathore sandalwood Pugal of the royal family, together with the royal sword, dagger and shield, in the City Palace at Bikaner. *See p. 47*

thousand inhabitants of the fortress, the heads of all the clans, and seventeen hundred of the ruler's 'immediate' relatives died on this occasion.

Meanwhile, during his few peaceful years of sovereignty, Udai Singh had dammed a valley about 112 kilometres from Chitor to form a lake connected to a second lake, the Pichola, created earlier by a fifteenth-century merchant to enable his pack animals to cross a stream. The many-storeyed, rambling City Palace of Udaipur now stands on the banks of the lake and formed the focal point of Udai's new capital.

Every Rajput state has witnessed similar dramatic episodes of treachery, intrigues and high courage. There was the Muslim servant who, in 1680, risked his life to carry to safety Ajit Singh, newly-born prince of Jodhpur, also hidden in a basket, this time of sweetmeats, after which the prince's mother and other female relatives were blown up; the tricking of the Hara chieftain into surrendering the great fortress of Ranthambhor to Akbar, who led the attack in person; and golden Jaisalmer's 'two-and-a-half' *jauhar*.

Bards still sing of the events that began with the ambushing of a treasure caravan of fifteen hundred horses and the same number of mules, winding across the arid desert to the king in Delhi. This probably took place about the end of the thirteenth century. Disguised as grain merchants, with seven thousand horses and twelve hundred camels, the Jaisalmer ruler's three sons killed the royal escort and triumphantly bore the king's tribute back to their desert capital. Learning that the king (probably Alauddin Khilji) was preparing a punitive expedition, Rawal Jethsi of Jaisalmer sent the elderly, the sick and the children of the city to safety in the desert, and then applied a scorched-earth policy to the surrounding country; he laid in immense stores of grain as well as great boulders at each of his fifty-six bastions, to be hurled on the heads of the attackers. The siege is said to have lasted for eight years and for two of those years the attackers themselves had their supply lines cut by the Rawal's grandson and great-grandson, Deoraj and Hamir, commanding the forces strategically left outside the fort.

During the siege Rawal Jethsi died, and his son Mulraj II ascended the *gadi*. At times, this was a very gentlemanly siege: for years Mulraj's brother, Ratansi, had been meeting the commander of the attacking force under a tree half-way between the two advance posts, where they would play chess; whenever there was a skirmish, the two men would forget their war game and fight in earnest. When the enemy was reinforced towards the end of 1294, Jaisalmer suffered a complete blockade, until both food and ammunition were practically exhausted. Ratansi had often been reproached for consorting with the enemy, but now he took the lead, suggesting that there was no alternative but to perform a *saka*.

All the chieftains agreed, and Mulraj and his brother told their queens of the decision that they should 'take the *sohag*', that is, become *sati* before their husbands' death. The women spent the night bathing, praying and dressing in their wedding finery, and at dawn twenty-four thousand of them died. It was impossible to construct a funeral pyre large enough to consume them all, so some were put to the sword by their male relations. Then, with the smell of burning flesh and freshly-spilled blood in their nostrils, the men donned their wedding robes over their armour, bound the *mor* (the glittering peacock coronet worn on two occasions only, marriage and death in battle),

80 The silver throne of the Jaipur maharajas with the ceremonial regalia, including flywhisks. City Palace, Jaipur

round their helmets together with a sprig of the *tulasi* (or *tulsi*, sacred basil) plant, symbolic of funerals, and the three thousand eight hundred warriors that had survived were ready for the final assault.

First, however, the laws of chivalry were invoked as Ratansi asked his former chess opponent to save the lives of his two sons, the eldest only eleven years old. The boys were escorted to the Muslim camp where the Nawab appointed two Brahmin priests to feed and instruct them. Then the *jauhar* began and both Jaisalmer brothers died with the flower of their armies.

In time the surviving Bhattis re-occupied Jaisalmer, repairing the damage and settling down, but it was not long before one of the princes daringly stole the prize stud of the then Sultan of Delhi, Jalauddin Firoz Shah, when the royal horses were being watered at Anasagar lake in Ajmer. No matter that Jaisalmer was surrounded by the Great Thar Desert, it was not remote enough to escape vengeance, and this time sixteen hundred women died and Rawal Dudu and his son Tilaski fell with seventeen hundred of their warriors. (Tod tells the story in graphic detail, together with equally dramatic histories of the other Rajput States.)

The handsome gate through which one passes today to reach the picturesque artificial lake of Gadi-Sar at the foot of Jaisalmer cliff was built by Telia, a favourite courtesan of one of the rulers. Generously she donated this to the people of Jaisalmer, but the ladies of the royal house were outraged at her presumption and threatened to demolish it. The quick-witted Telia immediately arranged for a statue of the deity Satya Narayan to be installed in a room above the gate, thus consecrating it as a temple to one of Vishnu's many aspects. As a shrine it could not be destroyed, but the royal family saved face by approaching the lake from another route, never passing through this obnoxious reminder of the upstart.

About the middle of the fifteenth century Rawal Chachakdeo captured the heads of three hundred and sixty-five wealthy Jain families from a local town, bankers and merchants, and held them to an unusual ransom. The price of their freedom was agreement to settle in Jaisalmer and it was this forcible settlement that eventually brought prosperity to the state.

The 'half' *jauhar* took place in the sixteenth century when a neighbouring chieftain from Afghanistan played a Trojan horse trick on Jaisalmer. His screened palanquins were supposed to be carrying his harem ladies to visit those of Jaisalmer but actually held armed men; however, the plan to capture the city without a battle failed. A hand-to-hand fight followed, and as it seemed a hopeless cause for the unprepared Jaisalmer defenders the Bhatti ruler killed his queens with his own hands – once again there was no time to prepare a funeral pyre. The horror of the Rawal can be imagined when before the ruler and his followers could carry out their part of the *jauhar*, rescue came in the shape of reinforcements, and the treacherous Pathan chieftain was blown to pieces by a cannon-ball. The women had died in vain, but their menfolk survived, hence the 'half' *jauhar*, fulfilling the ancient prophecy.

Jaisalmer's history of intrigue and murder in rivalry for the throne is as

81 The throne of the maharaja of Kota, covered by a canopy, Kota City Palace

bloodthirsty as that of other Rajput states, but one unforeseen result of the settlement of the *bania* merchants was their increasing influence over the Maharawal rulers. The Mehta family in particular became hereditary ministers of state, extremely powerful because it was their wealth that really supported Jaisalmer. During the eighteenth century the Prime Minister, Sarup Singh Mehta, was murdered by the Jaisalmer heir-apparent in a dispute over a maiden who preferred a Rajput to the Jain. It is also said that the *bania* had demanded payment of a loan, and was cut down by the infuriated prince whom he had accosted in public.

Whatever the cause, Sarup's eleven-year-old son Salim succeeded his father as Prime Minister and is described as being effeminate, bland, courteous – and completely insincere. Over the years he nursed such a terrible hatred of the ruler's family and determination for revenge that eventually he managed to destroy not only the family but Jaisalmer itself.

On the surface he appeared to be a weakling of no account, but by the time he reached manhood, most of the royal family was heavily in debt to him. Arson, poison and the dagger: the Mehta used them all in Borgia fashion to rid himself of any members of the ruling family or their loyal nobles who might question his powers. Those that remained could not order a new garment or jewels or even use their own horses without Salim Singh's permission. Eventually he even forced some five thousand of his own wealthy community to move away to escape his outrageous taxation, although he detained members of the richest families as hostages for further extortion.

Colonel Tod was Political Agent for Jaisalmer at this time, and saw how Rawal Gaj Singh, the ruler in name only from 1820 to 1846, was entirely isolated and dependent on Salim Singh even for his grudgingly fulfilled daily needs, with household spies reporting his every word and movement. Jaisalmer was the last of the princely states of Rajasthan to receive the protection of the British Government, and was an area difficult to defend because of its isolated desert frontiers, but vital in view of the threatened invasion from Russia and from Napoleon at that time.

Tod reported his disgust at the Mehta's behaviour, but in 1824, before anything could be done officially, a desperate Rajput stabbed the tyrannical Prime Minister and, as the historians of the time put it, 'since there was some fear that the wound might heal, his wife gave him poison'.

One of the sights of Jaisalmer today is Salim Singh's magnificent *haveli*, more of a self-contained residential complex than a mansion, with its elaborately carved, many-storeyed golden façade and balconies.

As in the other great fortified Rajput cities, one senses that the very stones refuse to be silent, crying out the dramas of the past. It takes little imagination to conjure up once again the fiery histories of the Rajput rulers and their courageous, lovely queens.

82 The Tower of the Winds at Jaipur City Palace: a building consisting only of a façade, behind which the ladies of the court could watch what went on in the city

CHAPTER TEN
The Supreme Sacrifice

Mass immolations at the time of a *jauhar* during warfare were not the only instances of wives preferring death to life without their husbands.

Rajasthan's fortresses and royal cemeteries are full of sad reminders of wives and concubines who regarded it as an honour and a joy to join their husbands' corpses on the funeral pyre. Set into the walls of many great castles are tiles bearing the palm impressions, painted vermilion, of queens and 'curtain wives of affection' who walked through those portals for the last time on their way to commit a fiery suicide.

These pathetic memorials testify to one of Rajasthan's most ancient and widespread customs, that of becoming a *sati*, literally, a 'virtuous woman'. There are nearly thirty scarlet palm impressions in Bikaner's sixteenth-century gateway, while no less than eighty-four women accompanied the body of the Bundi Maharaja who was drowned during the Gangaur festival in 1724. That same year, when the Jodhpur ruler Ajit Singh died, sixty-four women became *sati*.

According to the bardic account of that funeral: '... the Chauhani queen, with sixteen handmaidens, came out of her quarters saying, "This day is one of joy ... our lives have passed together, how then can I leave him?", and the Jaisalmir queen added, "with joy I accompany my lord ..."' The fifty-eight concubines, going joyfully to the funeral pyre, said that they would never have another such opportunity and that if they survived their lord, they would only become prey to disease and death at home. Alms were given 'like falling rain', while the countenances of the women, as they went in procession, were radiant as the sun.

The custom has a deep spiritual and social significance. The sacrifice of wives, personal servants, favourite horses (in fact of those closest and dearest to the dead man) to accompany him on his journey to the next world has been found all over the ancient world, but in India it seems to have lasted longer than most. Professor Romila Thapar thinks the origins of *sati* may lie in the symbolic self-immolation of Aryan widows during the Vedic period, and Colonel Tod traces the custom to 'sun-worshipping Saivas' and the Scythian practice by which the widow was consumed on the funeral pyre with her husband's body. Greek accounts of Alexander's invasion of India give the earliest datable mention of *satis*, when the fourth-century BC Seleucid leader Eumenes was killed and his funeral became the scene of a violent dispute between his wives as to which of them should claim the privilege of burning on his pyre.

The earliest known memorial to a *sati* is in two brief verses inscribed on a pillar carved in 510 AD at Eran, near Sagar, in Madhya Pradesh, bordering

83 The ramparts of the fortress of Chitor

Rajasthan. Bhanu Gupta, 'the bravest man on earth', was killed in battle and his wife, 'loyal, and loving, beloved and fair, followed close behind him into the flames'.

A Hindu widow could generally expect a miserable existence; no man would want to risk incurring the misfortunes attached to marriage with her. Stripped of all ornaments and jewels, wearing only the white garments of mourning, shunned even by the servants, and sleeping on the floor, the widow was allowed only one plain meal daily. Humiliated by her husband's family, who regarded her as being responsible for his death through a flaw in her own character, she could never take part in family festivals, for her mere presence would bring bad luck.

The wretched woman would more often than not prefer an 'honourable and memorable death', particularly if her husband had other wives and concubines prepared to become *sati*. In such circumstances psychological pressure to conform to custom would be almost irresistible, especially in the case of highborn Rajput women of the Kshatriya or warrior caste.

As long ago as the seventh century AD the poet Bana condemned the custom, while the tantric sects made a point of denouncing it, saying that such a woman was not to be admired but would be destined for hell. The Mughal Emperor Jahangir tried to abolish the tradition, specifically forbidding it to widows with young children and, later, any woman under compulsion, although that did not prevent the most determined Rajput queens from sacrificing their lives.

One story dramatically underlining the Rajput attitude to *sati* is told by Major John W. Watson in the August 1873 issue of *Indian Antiquary*; he relates how Hun, the last Raja of Chandravati in Jhalrapatan, witnessed the death of a tribal woman whose husband had died of a cobra-bite. She sliced off pieces of her own flesh, casting them on her husband's funeral pyre, before mounting the fire herself. Returning home, the Raja told his queen, Rani Pingla, of the woman's devotion, but the Rani maintained that the woman was not a true *sati* but a *surmi* (a brave or desperate character) who had destroyed herself on the spur of the moment.

She claimed that a real *sati* was one who, on even hearing of her husband's death, would bathe, clasp his turban to her breast, and heave such an immense sigh that the escape of the soul, shattering her skull, caused instant death.

Afterwards, fearful that her husband might one day put her to the test, the Rani consulted her Guru who told her to plant the seed of an *asso pal* tree. When the plant was mature she should ask it if her husband was indeed alive or dead; if he was alive the plant's leaves would ooze water, but if the Raja had died the plant would also die.

When eventually Raja Hun rode into battle, he did indeed test his wife by sending her a messenger bearing his turban, the sign of his death. The *asso pal* plant oozed water, confirming the queen's suspicions that her husband was testing her, but now she was in a dilemma: if she did not become *sati*, her husband would cease to love her and her father would be shamed. If she died, it would be a useless sacrifice, yet by doing so she would eventually be reunited with her husband in heaven and in their next rebirth on earth.

Rani Pingla explained all this to the plant, and then, clasping her

84 A carved image in a temple set deep into the walls of the Chitor fortress; although said by some to be the princess Padmini, it is in fact much earlier in style and is probably a deity

husband's turban to her breast, gave a huge sigh and died. When her distraught husband learnt the result of his deception he was overwhelmed with grief and remorse, and spent the rest of his life as a wandering holy man.

There was another type of memorial to ritual suicides besides the palm prints on gateway walls, and these were known as *paliya* or *jujhar* (sacrificial pillars). These memorials are uniquely Rajput and can probably be traced to Central Asian nomadic tribes. Some of the most touching *paliyas* are those of Bikaner in the royal cemetery at Devikund, where they are known as *devalis*, from the Sanskrit meaning 'a place of the gods'.

Here, in a charming, tree-shaded enclosure on the banks of an artificial lake, stand a group of dark red sandstone *chhatris*. *Chhatri* literally means 'umbrella' and the monuments are constructed with umbrella-shaped domes supported on slender carved columns, each set upon a plinth. The ashes of the deceased may or may not be buried under the funeral stones.

Maharaja Zorawar Singh's *chhatri* with its fluted columns on lotus bases shows the marble *paliya* stele in the centre, with the ruler depicted fully armed on his charger, an attendant holding the royal umbrella over his head, the sun and crescent moon above and four of his queens by his horse. Below, in two rows, are twenty-two other female images of *satis* with long skirts and demurely folded hands.

Another *paliya* depicts Anup Singh who died in 1698, also with the sun and moon, a royal umbrella held over his head and seven queens by his horse, ten other *satis* in a row below. And at Nagaur, once part of Bikaner State and now included in Jodhpur, a small *chhatri* next to that of Amar Singh has the impression of a pair of tiny feet carved from marble and set into the floor. Daily some unknown admirer lovingly places a garland of fresh marigolds around the footprints. This is not a *paliya* but another type of memorial, to Amar Singh's favourite young wife, with whom he dallied too long and at whose request his dead body was brought back from Agra.

Colonel Narain Singh, former controller of HH Bikaner's household and latterly in charge of the State Hotel which was the royal palace, knows all the old legends. He recounts how Aurangzeb had instructed Amar Singh's own brother-in-law to assassinate him after the amorous prince had overstayed his leave from the emperor's troops, unable to tear himself away from his new bride and the delightfully painted pavilions of Nagaur, which can still be seen.

When finally Amar Singh reluctantly returned to Agra, he was murdered for his disobedience. His bride begged a nobleman to bring her husband's corpse to Nagaur. After a spectacular escape from Agra, with his charger leaping over the walls of the Red Fort and breaking both forelegs in the effort, the rescuer seized another horse and continued the flight to Nagaur, bearing his prince's body. The widow was thus able to mount the funeral pyre with her husband's corpse in her arms.

Tod has a slightly different version, with Amar Singh's widow, a Bundi princess, personally bringing her husband's body from Agra, taking it through the Bokhara Gate, which was afterwards known as Amar Singh's Gate and closed permanently until a British Army Officer reopened it in 1809.

A widow following her husband to his grave after death is *Duhagan* but a

85 The small lake pavilion of Padmini, where she was said to have been sighted by Sultan Alauddin Khilji

Overleaf

86 The fire-blackened remains of the palace of Chitor, under which Padmini took her ladies to the *jauhar* funeral pyre *(Chapter 9)*

87 Palm-prints of ranis who became *sati*, with memorial inscriptions. Bikaner City Palace

wife who, anticipating his death in battle, becomes *sati* while her husband is still alive is *Sohagan*.

The reasons for such sacrifices have long ceased to exist and the coming of the British made it a criminal offence. But the plight of the high-caste Hindu widow, especially in a strictly conventional household, is often still unenviable. Even today one occasionally hears of such women resolutely attempting to become *sati*. Such a case was reported as recently as 1952 in Jodhpur on the death of the governor of the royal palace, General Jahan Singh. To the open admiration of a large crowd singing Vedic hymns in her honour, the General's widow succeeded in throwing herself on his funeral pyre and dying before the police managed to reach the scene.

The fearless lady was one of those welcoming the fiery death as a meritorious religious act which would reunite her eternally with her husband, a point of view which must explain, to a large extent, the extraordinarily long and firm hold this ancient custom has had on the peoples of Rajasthan.

And he fought a great and famous battle
and passed to heaven, a god among chieftains.
His wife, loyal and loving, beloved and fair,
Followed close behind him into the flames.

88 The cenotaphs of the ranis of
Jodhpur at Mandor

CHAPTER ELEVEN

The Princes & the Arts

With statues on the terraces
and Peacocks strutting by . . .
Kipling, *The Glory of the Garden*

Thanks largely to the princes of Rajasthan, India can boast some of the world's great artistic treasures. The Rajput courts, however small, vied with each other to produce the finest musicians, poets, architects, sculptors, artists and writers. Even though a prince was engaged in almost ceaseless battle with his neighbours or with invaders, his great concern was to develop his court into a centre of the arts, attracting the finest craftsmen available.

As the rulers' education broadened from studying the martial skills to an appreciation of the peaceful arts, so a genuine flowering of cultural activities made the courts of the Rajput princes some of the finest and most brilliant intellectual centres in all India. The part the princes played in encouraging the more sophisticated forms of music and dance was an important one, perhaps originating with the Charans and Bhatts who preserved the royal genealogies and heroic deeds in their poems and songs.

Dances originated in the temple offerings of ritual praises and music. In time the dancers, who were supported by the maharajas, would come to the palaces to entertain, and gradually their performances became more secular. Classical dancers require many years of arduous training, a fact which often makes royal patronage indispensable. Written nearly two thousand years ago, the Natya Shastra, a treatise on dancing, gave three distinct aspects to the dance: *nritta, nritya* and *natya. Nritta* is dance pure and simple, consisting of body movements performed for their own beauty and decorative effect. *Nritya* is essentially meant to convey the meaning of a theme through facial expressions, stylized hand gestures and symbolic body postures. *Natya*, in addition to the facial and hand expressions, introduces drama through the spoken word. Two more divisions are those of *tandava*, a bold and robust style, and *lasya*, tender and graceful. All these features are common to classical dances.

Jaipur has a Kathak (North Indian classical) school of its own, with a scintillating technique in pure dance form. Because the dance became popular at the Muslim courts, the accepted costume is Mughal – tight *churidar* pyjamas with a finely-pleated muslin skirt over them, and an almost transparent *kurta* or tunic worn with an embroidered velvet waistcoat and cap. The dances are often depicted in court miniatures which show Krishna himself wearing the Mughal dress.

89 Nineteenth-century painting of British representatives received by Maharana Swarup Singh of Udaipur, in the City Palace. The peacock illustrated on the cover can be seen on the left

Accompaniment to the dancers consists of drummers on a pair of small *tablas* and a *pakhavaj* (a double drum slung around the neck), a vocalist and an instrumentalist. Flutes (the nasal *shahnai*) and stringed instruments such as the *sitar* and *sarod*, plucked, and the *sarangi*, played with a bow, are added. *Bhopa* minstrels singing the *phad* stories use an antique single-stringed instrument, the *ravanhatha*.

Like dance, classical music evolved from the temples and Vedic hymns; the Vedas refer to God as 'The Dancer', 'The Poet', and 'The Singer'. Brahma's own consort Saraswati is portrayed holding a *vina*, a stringed instrument, while Shiva is a teacher of music and in South India, especially, is worshipped as Nataraja, Lord of the Dance.

The richness of Indian music is seen in its modes, twelve of them, one for every season, mood and occasion. In each of these there are *ragas* (melodies formed from five, six or seven notes) with extremely wide permutations of form in sharps, flats and trills and flurries, each used at specific times such as dawn, noon, dusk and nightfall, monsoon or hot weather, spring and winter – and these *ragas* are never used at any other time of day or season.

Gwalior, whose maharajas have always been outstanding patrons of music and where the famous singer Tansen, one of Akbar's 'Nine Jewels', is buried, is still an important musical centre and its *gharana* is the oldest of the many schools of Khayal singing. The Gwalior *gharana* is a type of open-throated singing, very formal and with simple transitions from note to note. The Jaipur-Atroli *gharana* is different, with a 'monumental weight', slightly slower in tempo than the other schools.

Other forms of vocal music derive from localities and occupations. For instance, the *tappa* is a development of the camel drivers' songs, but is now a classical style with fast turns of phrase. The *ghazal*, heard at all the Rajput courts right up to the present day, came from Persia and is a lyrical love song, now distinctly Indian.

Princely patronage extended to religious as well as secular art, and not only in supporting temples, dancers and singers. In commissioning the buildings themselves, the rulers would make sure of a place in heaven as well as perpetuating their own memory on earth. Marble sculptures of the deities and saints, carved with great delicacy and warmth, vie with the lacy marble filigree screens in the palaces, from behind which languishing princesses could glimpse their would-be suitors. By the seventeenth and eighteenth centuries, the courts of many Rajput rulers had become active centres of art.

Apart from the beauty of the palace architecture, the interior decoration is most striking. Bundi and Kota City Palaces have some outstanding murals in their Halls of Audience. Raja Satrusal of Bundi, who built the Rang Mahal in the seventeenth century, employed court artists to decorate his walls. A century later new subjects were introduced, such as royal processions and hunts. Raja Umed Singh probably employed some of the masters from the Jaipur courts and the walls of the Chatar Sali are covered with lively battle-scenes, charming pastorals, princesses in fancy dress as Mughal princes or hunting with falcons and sporting with bright green parrots. The predominant colours are cool turquoise, blue and green, matching the coolness of the central patio and its fountains. The later frescoes portray romantic landscapes with costumes in vivid colours, paying special attention

90 The interior of the main palace in Jodhpur fort: a mirrored ceiling with an eighteenth-century painting of angels

to details of background, perspective and architecture, and depicting more realistic figures.

When Rudyard Kipling was in Bundi in 1887 he watched artists painting wall-panels in the Rang Mahal in polychrome. Skirting the floor were the original seventeenth-century murals in red, black and white, depicting battles with elephants, much worn and defaced but of such a high standard as to put the later work to shame.

In Kota's own seventeenth-century City Palace, murals in the Raj Mahal Durbar Hall show single figures on a much larger scale, with long-nosed Rajput ladies solemnly accompanying their singing on musical instruments. Scenes from the Krishna-Lila epics and bird's-eye views of the palaces decorate the walls behind the scarlet throne.

Both Bundi and Kota artists were strongly influenced by the Mughal style, which in turn derived inspiration from the Persian masters, for the Safavid court artists and poets were much in demand at the Mughal courts of the sixteenth to eighteenth centuries. Among the famous *ustads* or masters who directly influenced Rajput painting were Jahangir's favourite, Manohar, son of Basawan, one of Akbar's greatest artists; Mansur, famed for his bird and animal paintings and given the title of Nadir-ul Asr (Wonder of the Time); and Abu-al Hasan, honoured with the title of Nadir-ul Zaman (Wonder of the Age) for his perfection in painting Jahangir's accession as the frontispiece to his memoirs. One masterpiece of the early seventeenth century, attributed to Govardhan, is an exquisitely detailed miniature showing Jahangir at Ajmer distributing food to the poor, with the tomb of Khwaja Chishti in the background – every one of the forty-nine persons shown is a faithful portrait.

Rajput artists outlined the face in profile and Stella Kramrisch traces the beginnings of Rajput art to classical painting during the period of its disintegration and re-absorption into folk art, as well as to the princes' rivalry with their Mughal overlords. The various schools of painting were developed purely for the delight of their princely patrons and Rajput murals, as she points out, seem like enlargements from an album.

Eighteenth-century Bundi painting distilled the essence of Indian art and, with the Kota school, is distinguished by its love of bright turquoise. The same period in Kota under the patronage of Rao Raja Umed Singh shows very strongly the influence of Bundi. The passion of the rulers for the hunt was depicted in a strong, simplified style.

William Archer points out that the Kota school – not even recognized until 1952 – revealed totally new concepts, involving 'trees, rocks and tigers subtly altered into something rich and strange with all attempts at realism abandoned ... the result is an art unique in Indian painting and one for which the only western parallel is that of the modern French artist Douanier Rousseau.'

Other smaller Rajput states developed distinctive schools through the patronage of their rulers. Kishangarh emerged in the eighteenth century under Raja Savant Singh, whose court artist, Nihal Chand, immortalized the romance of the ruler and Bani Thani, a famous beauty. The two are depicted in the roles of Radha and Krishna (Kishangarh rulers were devotees of Krishna) and other poetic lovers. Bani Thani is shown with tiny waist and

91 Jantar Mantar, the famous observatory built by the Maharaja Jai Singh at Jaipur

slender fingers, enormous eyes and curved eyebrows, a charming, languorous, fragile damsel.

Alwar, another small state, developed a more sophisticated style with, surprisingly enough, some very lovely nudes. Clad or nude, the ladies were always shown against stylized backgrounds.

Bikaner in the seventeenth and eighteenth centuries was also influenced by Mughal court artists, and is regarded as the most subtle and refined of Rajput schools, in which textures of materials are skilfully rendered, the colours subdued and warm. There are some outstanding examples in the Lalgarh Palace and a particularly good one is the portrait of Maharaja Kesari Singh on horseback, spearing a lioness.

The rulers of Bikaner and Jodhpur were especially noted for their patronage of the arts, the style being exceptionally delicate. The exterior walls of Bikaner's Karan Mahal are painted with such skill that, even close up, they deceive you into thinking they are of *pietra dura* inlaid with semi-precious stones, like the Taj Mahal. They are not even marble but lime plaster, highly polished with shells. The eighteenth-century Phool Mahal is elaborately decorated with inlaid mirrorwork over walls and ceiling, including the Maharaja's bedroom, while scenes of polo and hunting cover the walls of the galleries around it. The ceilings of the Diwan-i-Am and Diwan-i-Khas are enlargements of Persian miniatures, lavishly covered with gold leaf. A bedroom in the Moon Palace with stained-glass windows features beautifully painted wooden doors with lines of ducks around the base, and lively games of polo on the panels. And, keeping up the tradition in the nineteenth century, a frieze of Stephenson-type open railway carriages with Mughal canopies and funnelled steam engine is painted high on the walls of an inner courtyard.

The Phool Mahal of Jodhpur's City Palace, built by Raja Abhai Singh in the early eighteenth century, is a fairytale structure with jewel-like stained-glass windows in golden filigree; gold-painted abstract designs on ceiling and walls frame delicate miniatures.

At Nagaur the massive double-walled Mughal fort, where Akbar once stayed, contains several forlorn and neglected gems of palaces set in once-elaborate formal gardens. Until recently the charming pavilions where Raja Amar Singh dallied with his new bride were occupied by the military, who plastered over the delightful murals that have now been revealed. Panels on exterior walls are painted in typically Persian style with peacock-feathers and cypress trees. Stylized dancers and flowers are framed here and there, and inside, more frescoes adorn the rooms with their marble channels set into the walls and floors to conduct streams of scented water to cool the occupants.

The Mewars of Udaipur were the first to develop an indigenous school of painting in the fifteenth century from what had begun in nearby Gujarat with illustrated palm-leaf manuscripts. In the following two centuries this became a lively, colourful art form in which brilliant scarlets and vermilions, golden yellow and rich lapis lazuli reflected the tastes of the Ranas. Mewar artists were less inspired by the Mughal court than those of most other Rajput states, but the Mughal influence can certainly be seen on the charming little pavilions on Jag Mandir island, where Prince Khurram (to become Shah Jahan) found refuge from his father's anger in 1623. The domed, sandstone palace is decorated with the same type of fine marble, inlaid with onyx, cornelian, jasper and agate, as the later Agra palaces. The interior walls of the small pleasure pavilions feature the brilliant turquoise backgrounds of the Bundi-Kota schools with nobles and courtiers, elephants and other wild animals, while living birds flutter through the windows to settle on ledges by their painted counterparts.

Prince Khurram's host Maharana Karan Singh was responsible for the renaissance of art in Mewar. He began constructing his palaces just when other Rajput courts were adopting the Mughal style of the earlier reigns of Akbar and Jahangir, and it is likely that the Udaipur ruler employed the old-fashioned architects dismissed by the more up-to-date princes; the Udaipur City palaces thus retain the delightful, truly Rajput atmosphere.

Two hundred and twenty-four years after Prince Khurram enjoyed the hospitality of Jag Mandir, the same palaces in 1857 were to house a number of European families when Maharana Swaroop Singh offered protection to the women and children fleeing from Neemuch during the Sepoy uprising. The Maharana's reception of the British refugees, or rather, their male representatives, is the subject of a contemporary painting in the Udaipur City Palace.

Karan Singh and his son Jagat Singh I encouraged the rebirth of Rajput art, and Rana Raj Singh, Karan's grandson, was also a great patron of art and literature. But in 1662 a disastrous famine caused immense damage to the country. It was followed by political tensions at the Mughal court and a Mughal invasion in 1668 – a series of upheavals that for a time brought to a standstill any revival of the arts.

The early eighteenth century saw the more rapid economic disintegration of the Mughal Empire when Mewar, with other states, regained her independence, and the Rajput rulers lost no time in setting up splendid courts to rival those of the Mughals.

Artists trained at the Delhi courts now found themselves without commissions and were only too glad to migrate to the Rajput courts. Jagat Singh II, who died in 1752 aged only eighteen, spent the equivalent of a quarter of a million pounds sterling building and adding to the pavilions on the islands in Pichola Lake, employing many of the Delhi artists. What Dr Herman Goetz has described as the Mughal-Rajput style came into being 'in all its strength, in all its perfection of line, but also in its undeniable flatness of treatment'. The next ruler, Sangram Singh II, saw the end of the transition period and the emergence of a new, peculiarly Mewar Rajput style both in architecture and painting. Until the present day, Udaipur was to be the guardian of the Rajput traditions of art.

A small palace built in Jaipur for a Sisodia (Udaipur) princess, married to Maharaja Sawai Jai Singh II of Jaipur, has a fascinating series of murals all over its exterior. The palace and its formal gardens are on the road to Galta, a narrow gorge filled with temples (including one to the sun), all built round natural, healing springs where peacocks strut beneath the trees. The whole upper storey of the Sisodia Rani ka Bagh, which is crowned with domed and canopied pavilions, and is still used to entertain state guests, is covered with charming, vivid scenes: lovers strolling in gardens, gallants playing polo or hunting, elephants, battles and extraordinary mythical creatures.

Relations between Mewar and Jaipur had long been strained and the marriage was a political one. The unhappy Sisodia princess found that she was barely tolerated in the Maharaja's palace, and to make matters worse Jai Singh was suffering from an unpleasant skin disease. The powerful Mewar Sisodias had insisted that any son borne by their daughter should succeed to the *gadi*, so when she gave birth to a boy, Madho Singh, the Rani had this charming palace built well away from the city intrigues. (When Jai Singh died in 1743, his eldest son, Iswan Singh, and not Madho, succeeded, and it was only after seventeen years of fighting for his rights that Madho Singh eventually gained the throne.)

In spite of his unfortunate ailment, Jai Singh was really an attractive character and more than any other prince his personal contribution to the arts and sciences was exceptional. He was extremely intelligent, a scholar of Sanskrit and Persian, a scientist, mathematician and astronomer, not content to accept established theories but a talented inventor and researcher. He was only thirteen when he devised an ingenious irrigation system to water the hanging gardens of Amber. Some time after he came to the throne in 1699 he decided to move his capital from the fortified gorge of Amber, where his ancestors had lived for nearly six centuries, to the open plains. The foundations of this ultra-modern city of Jaipur were laid in 1727. It is designed in rectangular blocks, with the main streets more than thirty-three metres wide, and it is surrounded by a crenellated wall. Jaipur's buildings today are uniformly rose pink, compounded of white lime and powdered, underburnt terracotta. The colour was chosen after much experimentation with white, green and yellow, to cut down the intense glare from the reflection of the fierce sun.

Jai Singh studied the architecture of famous European cities, and consulted his foremost mathematicians, astronomers and the Shilpa Shastras, traditional Hindu treatises, before making the blueprint for the new capital. In his City Palace one can now see the tremendous range of miniature paintings developed in Jaipur, from some almost surrealist illustrated manuscripts of the Puranas to Mughal portraits, court, battle and processional scenes. The Jaipur school is noted for its sophistication and lavish use of gold. The walls and ceilings of some of the chambers are covered with floral motifs like those of a Persian carpet in soft creams, dark blue, russets and greens, richly ornamented, with pure gold settings for portraits of the various rulers painted onto the walls.

Outstanding examples of Rajasthan art – sculpture, jewellery, enamelware, paintings, carpets and some fifty thousand ancient manuscripts preserved from the ruling family's private collection – are on view in the oldest of the city palaces, the Chandra Mahal, converted to a museum by the Maharani Gayatri Devi when the old family home of Rambagh became a hotel.

Of all Jai Singh's achievements, the most famous are his five observatories, the largest of which, the Jantar Mantar, is in Jaipur City. Jai Singh was an unusually gifted astronomer and wanted to check personally the observations established in the fifteenth century by Uleg Beg and other Timurid astronomers of Samarkand. He corrected many long-accepted faulty calculations and was entrusted by the Emperor Muhammad Shah to

92 Balconies along the main entrance façade of Udaipur City Palace

reform the calendar. Since the bronze astrolabes in current use were not sufficiently accurate, Jai Singh invented his own gigantic instruments, fashioned of marble and stone, and erected his observatory even before his new capital was built. The result is the extraordinary, amazingly accurate collection of almost futuristic appearance where the royal inventor spent many hours in heavenly exploration.

Jai Singh gained a new title, that of *Sawai* (one and a quarter times), when he ascended the throne and, following tradition, paid his respects to the Emperor Aurangzeb in Delhi. The prince raised his hands to proffer his gifts but Aurangzeb flew into an unexpected rage, jumping from his throne to shout, 'Your ancestors gave us much trouble and were disloyal. Now, say what you deserve of me before saying what you desire.'

As Jai Singh stood speechless with astonishment, the emperor grasped both his outstretched hands in his own right hand and went on, 'Tell me, what use are your arms now?'

The young prince replied calmly, 'Your Imperial Majesty, during a wedding the bridegroom takes the bride's hand in one of his own and he is duty-bound to protect her for life. Now that the Emperor of India has taken my two hands in his, what have I to fear? With Your Majesty's long arms to protect me, what other arms do I stand in need of?'

Aurangzeb was so impressed by the prince's presence of mind that he said, 'You excel your ancestor Jai Singh in intelligence and ability. Indeed, you are *Sawai* Jai Singh (one and a quarter times Jai Singh) – let this then be the title for you and your successors.'

Many Rajput palaces boast mirror rooms, and among the finest are those in Amber and the City Palace where Sawai Madho Singh II completely covered his apartment in faceted mirrors, believing that they would frighten away the evil spirits. This prince, whose father died in 1835 when he was only eighteen months old, fled with his mother to the jungle when his youngest brother Ram was chosen to succeed. For forty-five years he lived as a bandit, until a holy man prophesied that he would become the Maharaja provided he led a pious life. Sure enough, when his half-brother died without an heir in 1880, Madho did succeed to the throne and continued to lead a strictly religious existence. He was present at the coronation of King Edward VII in 1901, and for the voyage to England hired an entire liner, taking sufficient holy water from the Ganges to bathe in it every day for six months!

Architecture of various kinds owes much to the patronage of the princes, not least their personal temples, their cenotaphs and some of the wonderful *baolis* or step wells, utilitarian structures yet superb examples of art. One of the finest is the Raniji ki Baoli in Bundi.

This well, forty-six metres in depth, is on the outskirts of the city. A row of small shops and restaurants is built into its upper wall, their kitchen waste now disfiguring the pale honey-coloured stone. The well was constructed for the benefit of travellers as well as of the people of Bundi, by a Solanki princess who was a junior Rani of Bundi. The young princess was a beauty and of royal blood but she was virtually penniless when she married the Bundi ruler, whose senior queen had been unable to produce the essential heirs. The new princess was lucky first time and gave the Maharao Raja his

93 The interior of Udaipur City Palace: mirrored and painted rooms, and windows with cut-out panels of coloured glass

longed-for son, but then the young woman's life was made wretched by the jealousy of the older queen. Finally the Solanki princess handed her son to the senior Rani and devoted herself to charitable works.

Her *baoli* was no ordinary one. A wide flight of steps leads through a triple archway – a *torana* – with a frieze of elephants, while two more stone elephants are half-submerged at the water level, together with an image of Ganesha, still serving as an active shrine. Into the walls are set delicate carvings of various deities including the goddess Mataji, surmounted by *sikaras* and domes, while the balconies and columns of the *torana* are also covered with fine tracery.

As for the *chhatris*, every state boasts its royal garden in which stand monuments to the dead monarchs. Udaipur's nineteen *chhatris* of white marble are built on high platforms within a walled enclosure, each with an image of Shiva and a *paliya* showing the Maharana and his *satis*. A stroll here at sunset with the prehistoric Ahar excavations in the background, the priest of the Shiva temple in his scarlet *lungi* and the silvery rays of the rising moon mingling with those of the setting sun, drenching the marble domes in magical tints, can be an experience transporting the visitor to past ages.

Jaipur's *chhatris* at Gaitor are also of white marble, and Sawai Jai Singh's, whose large dome is supported by twenty columns, has some exquisitely carved panels with stirring scenes of lion-hunts. His son Madho's cenotaph, with eight pillars, features peacocks on its marble base, while completely in keeping with those of his ancestors is the newest marble *chhatri* of the late Maharaja Sawai Man Singh (Jai), who died in 1970 after a fall from his pony during a polo match in England.

The majority of Bikaner's *chhatris* were constructed about eight kilometres from the city, near a large tank called the Devi Kund. Within the main enclosure stand the later memorials, and when the wall surrounding these was originally built it was foretold that all the succeeding rulers would be buried within it. Today, with the tomb of the last Maharaja, Badul Singh, erected there in 1950, the enclosure is full, and there are no more Maharajas.

Kota rulers' impressive *chhatris* are to be found in gardens on the edge of the fourteenth-century Bara Talao tank round which the city is built. On either side of a modern road cut through the gardens are the massive pavilions, some with life-sized stone elephants keeping guard. And tethered among the trees, a score or more enormous living elephants munch their way through piles of grass. Their owners, itinerant holy men, have set up house inside the *chhatris*, which are now adorned with lines of ragged washing and the debris of temporary squatters.

Does the end of the princes mean the end of artistic development in Rajasthan? Let us hope not. Whatever their titles or lack of them today, many of the former princes will continue to show an active interest in their hereditary lands and peoples, and it might even be that with the growing interest in Rajasthan shown by increasing numbers of foreigners, Rajput artists and craftsmen will give birth to yet fresh forms of artistic expression.

94 The step well *(baoli)* outside the city walls of Bundi

CHAPTER TWELVE
Princes & Palaces

If our poets had sung them,
our painters pictured them,
our heroes and famous men had lived in them,
their romantic beauty would be on every man's lips in Europe . . .
Ernest Havell, 1890, on Rajput Palaces

Rajput princes were tireless builders of castles and palaces, creating some of the most magnificent in the world, a great many of which are still in use today.

Their histories are full of romance and tragedy, like those of their originators. One of the most attractive of the many garden terraces of Udaipur's City Palace, open to the public, is the Mor Chowk or Peacock Court whose mosaic reliefs of dancing peacocks were added by the Maharana Sajjan Singh in the nineteenth century. Nearby is the famous Sun Window where the Maharanas, descendants of the Sun God himself, showed themselves to their people in times of misfortune, displaying the 'Rays of the Sun' as reassurance. By the balconied window are delightful glass mosaics of two eighteenth-century British noblemen with a pair of charming Rajput girls bearing trays of wine.

The wall of the porticoed Chholu Chattar Sali bears the dazzling dynastic symbol of the Mewars, with its moustachioed Rajput face and its rays of shining sword-blades surrounding the great golden sun, crowned with peacock feathers. The huge sun is flanked by two pairs of Rajput maidens waving the royal peacock feathers and yak-tail fans, and dates from the time of Maharana Karan Singh, who built the pavilion in 1620. To one side of the porch hangs a fascinating painting of Colonel James Tod complete with cocked hat and dress coat, accompanied by six Europeans, being received in audience by Maharana Bhim Singh in the same court, in 1818 *(see p.41)*.

That was the year that Tod was appointed Political Agent to Udaipur and formally presented his credentials to the Court. The Maharana's gift, as custom decreed, included a caparisoned elephant and a horse, jewelled aigrette and pearl necklace, shawls and brocades. But this was not a one-sided transaction. Shortly afterwards the Maharana paid a return visit to Tod who then made his official Government presentations of an elephant and *two* horses, all caparisoned in silver, gilt and velvet, plus twenty-one shields

95 The seventeenth-century Udaipur Lake Palace, today a luxurious hotel, seen from Jagmandir Island on Lake Pichola

laden with fine shawls of honour, brocades, muslins and jewels. Similar gifts and horses were given to the Rana's sons and brothers and the chief court ministers.

At this time Mewar was in a very poor economic situation and it was only the generosity of the Maharao Zalim Singh of Kota that enabled the Udaipur ruler to live with any degree of comfort. It was at this stage that Udaipur signed a treaty with the British and, with Colonel Tod's able administration, was restored to prosperity.

In his travel book *From Sea to Sea*, Rudyard Kipling describes his experiences in Rajasthan when he was a twenty-two-year-old reporter. He made a special note of the various state crests. Udaipur's shield – 'gules and a sun in splendour' – had as its crest the straight, double-edged Rajput sword known as the Khandra, supported by a Bhil and a Rajput in his *jauhar* dress, reminders of the sieges of Chitor and of the Mewar founder's debt to the tribal chieftains.

The enormous palace is really a whole series of mansions, constructed at different periods since Udai Singh laid its foundations in the sixteenth century. Following the traditional origins of most royal residences the story goes that he was hunting along the shores of Pichola when he came across a holy man and paused to pay his respects. The hermit advised Udai Singh to build a palace around this very spot and good fortune would then follow. The prince began by erecting a small shrine, now incorporated in the palace and one of the first chambers the visitor sees. Paintings of the four chief Mewar deities, Charbhuja, Eklingji, Shri Nathji and Amba Mata, line the walls, while a wooden railing encloses the spot where Udai Singh discovered the sage.

Seen from the Lake Palace floating on Pichola, the City Palace rises storey upon forbidding storey, fronting the lake, a great white fortress topped by domed pavilions and cupolas at different levels. But inside, the atmosphere is generally one of spaciousness and airiness in a bewildering variety of individual palaces, gardens and courtyards. The charming Chini Chitrashala with its cool blue and white Chinese and Delft tiles includes scenes of Joseph and Mary with the Infant Jesus on their flight into Egypt. A raised, tiled platform provides an aerial view of the lake through delicately scalloped arches, while one end of the dais with its Christian motif gives onto a temple to Lord Shiva.

One of the palace suites, the Krishna Vilas, with its many fine miniature paintings, was the scene of a tragedy in the reign of Bhim Singh, in 1806. At that time Mewar was already surrounded by enemies, including the powerful rulers of Jodhpur and Jaipur, both of whom wanted to marry Bhim Singh's lovely sixteen-year-old daughter, Krishna Kumari. The Maharana was afraid of offending either prince, yet lacked the courage or the means to refuse them. It was the young princess herself who solved the dilemma by resolutely drinking a cup of poison in this apartment, which was her private suite. Soon after her daughter's suicide, her mother followed her example, and Bhim Singh, full of belated regrets, turned the Krishna Vilas into a shrine commemorating the women's courage.

But it is Udaipur's lake palaces that are her glory. The Jagnivas, built in the seventeenth century by Maharana Jagat Singh of granite and white

96 A view of the lake palace from the sixteenth-century City Palace, Udaipur

marble on four acres of rock, seemingly floats before the City Palace. Now it is the Lake Palace Hotel, one of the most romantic and luxurious hotels in the world, its delicate pavilions mirrored in the still waters of Pichola, with delightful interior gardens, fountains and pools, hidden courtyards, suites furnished in truly royal style and, a new addition not thought of by the originators, a swimming-pool. The last Maharana, Bhagwat Singh, decided to turn some of his ancestral palaces into hotels as long ago as 1956. The former Household Transport Centre on the banks of the lake opposite the Lake Palace Hotel was opened in 1963 as the Garden Motel, designed mainly for pilgrims to the shrines around the city. The same year the Lake Palace was opened to a more cosmopolitan clientèle, while a third island palace, perhaps by association the most romantic of all, on Jag Mandir Islet, is scheduled for development. Jag Mandir was begun by Maharana Karan Singh in the early seventeenth century and named for his heir, Prince Jagat Singh I. It was there that Prince Khurram lived in comfortable exile after a quarrel with his father, the Emperor Jahangir.

One can picture the royal prince on this enchanted islet with its pools of lotuses, its balustrade of trumpeting elephants (although these may have been added later), and the charming, now somewhat forlorn little pavilions. And it was here that the prince was first acclaimed as the Emperor Shah Jahan on the death of his father.

Prince Khurram is also remembered in the heraldry of the fairytale state of Bundi. The Mughal prince was trying to raise Rajasthan against his father (the eventual cause of his later exile). Twenty-two Rajput princes supported his rebellion, but not Rao Ratan of Bundi. In 1579 he defeated Khurram in a battle at Burhanpur, where his two sons were both severely wounded. Jahangir rewarded Bundi with the government of Burhanpur, granted Kota city and its dependencies to his second son Madho, and a little later, when Rao Ratan captured a noted rebel nobleman, granted the Bundi ruler the honour of having kettle-drums, a grand yellow banner to be carried before him in processions, and a red flag for his camp, all of them much-sought-after honours. The coat of arms appears to commemorate these events, with what Kipling described as a 'demi-god' of sable on a gold field, surrounded by flames and holding a sword in his right hand and a bow in the left. The diamond-hilted sword in its red velvet scabbard, the shield and dagger are still the Bundi symbols of state.

Kipling's initial experiences in Bundi were not happy. At the time of his visit, Englishmen were not made welcome. After a long and trying drive in a *tonga* (a one-horse carriage) over a hundred and twenty kilometres along rough, dusty roads, the young reporter arrived at the city gates to find he was not allowed to stay in the city but must continue to the Surkh Mahal, further along the banks of the Bara Talao. The pillared pavilion stands today, reflected in the lake where Bhil men and women energetically do their washing on the *dhobi* ghats, while along the shores graceful Bhil girls in striking scarlet and yellow skirts carry long bundles of firewood on their heads.

Kipling was housed in the colonnade 'open to the winds of heaven, and the pigeons of the Raja. But the latter had polluted more than the first could purify.' After hours of waiting, exhausted and hungry, he finally got two

A horse of wood
Legs of stone
A frame of iron
Alone get you to Jaisalmer.
Local quatrain

97 The ramparts of the fortress of Jaisalmer, in the far west of Rajasthan

youths to wind some canvas inexpertly round the columns to make a kind of loosebox, where he slept in considerable discomfort. Despite this unfortunate beginning and the fact that he was accompanied everywhere by at least two unhelpful armed guards, Kipling eventually fell in love with Bundi. 'It is a beautifully lazy city, doing everything in the real, true, original native way, and it is kept in very good order by the Durbar (Government) ... a jumbled city of straight streets, cool gardens where gigantic mangoes and peepuls intertwine over gurgling water courses and the cuckoo comes out at midday ...'

Bundi today is still an experience which memory enhances. I have never forgotten the enchantment of a royal party to celebrate the skilful modernization of the Moti Mahal, an old palace on the shores of the Naval Sagar, in the 1940s: soft lights reflected in the still waters, a full moon illuminating the rooftop celebrations, a splendid dance band on one flat roof, while on another the handsome young Maharao Raja, superb sportsman, distinguished soldier and ADC to King George VI, encouraged a Gurkha pipe-major in his enthusiastic rendering of Highland laments.

And when the dancing-girls appeared, a memorable moment was the whispered admonition to pay great respect to the most mature of them all, whose years fell away miraculously as she whirled and danced to the beat of the *tabla* and the plucking of *sitar* strings, 'because she was my grandfather's favourite!'

The Moti Mahal is still there with its overgrown creepers, concealing trees and screeching peacocks. Dominating the lake palace and the half-submerged temple to Varuna, the Aryan God of Wind, are the labyrinthine terraces and massive outer walls of that extraordinary collection of royal buildings begun in 1580 by Maharao Raja Balwant Singh, shimmering under a blazing sun and almost the same colour as the pink rocky hillside into which it blends.

It was the palace of Bundi, climbing up the steep hillside, that so captured Kipling's imagination, as it does today's visitor. Kipling wrote, 'Whoever has seen the Palace of Boondi can easily picture to himself the hanging gardens of Semiramis ... to give on paper any adequate idea of the Boondi-ka Mahal is impossible. Jeypore palace may be called the Versailles of India. Udaypoor's House of State is dwarfed by the hills around it, and the spread of the Pichola Lake. Jodhpur's House of Strife, grey towers on red rock, is the work of giants, but the Palace of Boondi even in broad daylight is such a palace as men build for themselves in uneasy dreams – the work of goblins rather than of men.'

The steep climb from the outer Hazari Pol gateway to the Hathi Pol, where two fighting elephants carved in black stone engage in perpetual battle over the gateway bearing their name, is overlooked by the protruding lattice windows and arched balconies of the palace. Panels of dancing peacocks decorate the flanking towers, while the cool shadows of the deep arch shelter an ancient water-clock, still in use, whose almost equally ancient keeper strikes a metal gong every half-hour.

98 The yellow sandstone ramparts of the twelfth-century fortress of Jaisalmer

The inner courtyard, with its Hall of Public Audience, is surrounded by stables over which is the Raj Mahal, a covered gallery with a balcony. In it there is a ghostly white marble throne where the rulers of Bundi were installed at their coronations. Here, in 1820, Colonel Tod assumed the guardianship of the eleven-year-old Maharao Ram Singh after his father, dying of cholera, entrusted the heir to the British Agent.

Tod describes the complicated purification rites preceding the investiture and how he was instructed to lead the young prince to the marble throne, dip his finger into a mixture of sandalwood powder and aromatic oils, and mark his forehead with the *tilak*. Then he bound the State Sword around his waist and formally announced the British Government's abiding interest in the ruler's welfare. The prince was then presented with the Government's many gifts, including jewels, richly caparisoned horses and an elephant.

The mother of the new young ruler, a Rathore princess from Kishangarh, sent Colonel Tod the *rakhi* bracelet, thereby adopting him as her 'brother', and making Tod the boy's 'uncle' and protector. This was followed by a three-hour conversation held with a curtain between them to conceal the Rani, whom Tod found to be extremely knowledgeable about government affairs, 'sensible and forthright'.

Bundi palace's terraces support pavilions adorned with delicate murals, lush gardens with mature cypress, orange and myrtle trees, fountains and pools. There are deep dungeons, and granaries which in the late fifteenth century Rao Banda filled with grain, so that during a severe famine some years later he was able to distribute it freely to the population, saving them from starvation. Later the ruler's two youngest brothers embraced Islam and sent their brother into exile while they jointly ruled Bundi. It was Banda's son, Narayandas, grown to manhood in exile, who after his father's death set out with a small band of loyal Haras to take his rightful heritage. Following the usual period of mourning for his father, he sent a message to his Muslim uncles requesting permission to pay his respects. He was allowed to enter the lower Hazari Pol, where he left his followers in the cobbled square and climbed alone up the steep, dog-legged approach to the Hathi Pol. Armed with his double-edged *khanda* sword and a lance, the prince approached his two uncles who, after eleven years of undisputed rule, felt secure enough to await him almost unattended. As soon as they saw his expression the brothers made for a secret passage and safety. But Narayandas was faster and killed one with a blow of his sword and speared the other.

As Kipling observed, although all Indian palaces are 'full of eyes', the feeling of being watched in Bundi palace is overpowering. 'There were trap doors on the tops of terraces, windows veiled in foliage and bulls' eyes set low in unexpected walls, and many other peepholes and places of vantage.'

Only when he viewed the full extent of the palace from across the valley did Kipling realize he had not seen a tenth of it. But even after his cold reception and dismal first impressions he 'had fallen in love with Boondi the beautiful' and believed he would 'never again see anything half so fair'.

In 1912, while the King-Emperor George V was in Nepal, Queen Mary visited her good friend the Maharao of Bundi, who gave strict instructions that no man should dare to look upon the great Queen-Empress on pain of

99 The marble throne in the Hall of Public Audience, Bundi Palace, where the maharaos were invested, now ghostly under dust-sheets

severe punishment. Save for the Maharao, not a man was in sight for the whole of her visit.

The younger Hara state of neighbouring Kota has its capital on the banks of the fast-flowing Chambal, with its whirlpools and rapids. It is now harnessed by the Kota barrage and other dams which serve six power-plants, including an atomic power-station for nuclear research. The old city palace, overlooking the river and enclosed within stout, crenellated walls pierced by the Suraj Pol with the rounded sun symbols, is redolent of the state's proud history. The early-seventeenth-century Raj Mahal is named for Rao Madho Singh, founder of Kota, who proved his courage and daring in 1579/80 when he was only fourteen. In years to come, Madho's five sons all donned the saffron robes and wedding crowns of peacock feathers denoting death or victory, to lead their vassals in a forlorn battle on behalf of the ageing Emperor Shah Jahan, whose son Aurangzeb usurped his father's throne. All five Kota princes fell on the field but the youngest, Kishor Singh, although severely wounded, survived, to distinguish himself in many future battles. When he died the scars of fifty wounds were counted on his body.

The Throne-Room, with its gold lion-headed mace and Sword of State, insignia of royalty which the Maharao would carry into battle or hold when giving audience, together with the peacock fan (the *morchal*) waved over his head, a bow and arrow, quiver and a round gold standard with red, blue and green silk banners, are reminders of the not so distant pageantry of the past.

In the river below the palace, enormous muggers, man-eating crocodiles, fat and lazy, would doze on the sandbanks. Until recent times a palace servant in his huge red turban daily called the individual creatures by name to a jetty. The muggers responded by clambering out of the river and up the steps to receive their ration of goat meat. The crocodiles have disappeared with the coming of the industrial projects, while the royal hunting-grounds on the outskirts of the city, where only a few years ago the Maharao's lavish shoots would end with even more lavish picnics, have given way to workers' housing settlements.

Along the road from Kota to Palaitha castle (the seat of a younger branch of the Hara family) and Gwalior is a small but important bridge whose worn inscription states that Colonel Tod had it constructed in 1818, financed by loot captured from local bandits.

There are said to be more nobles and wealthy landed proprietors in Jaipur than in any other state except Hyderabad, Deccan. And some, like Khetri and Sikar, were semi-independent, every one of them boasting numerous castles and palaces. But of them all, the royal fortified palace in Amber is the most romantic. Originally the capital of the Mina tribal territory, Amber was founded in the eleventh century. Approached through a narrow cleft in the rocky Aravalli Hills about eleven kilometres from the present city of Jaipur, it surmounts a steep cliff, its towers and white walls reflected in a small lake, its long, russet-gold ramparts snaking up the cliff and along the summit. The old capital takes its name from Amba Mata, the fertility and earth-goddess of the Minas – or, as some think, from Ambikeswara, one of Shiva's titles. There is a partially submerged stone *lingam* in the lake at the foot of the cliff, and an old tradition maintains that when this is fully submerged the state of Amber will perish.

100 The ramparts and palace of Jodhpur fort

Everything is geared to elephant transport. Wide platforms and domed pavilions are just the right height for travellers to step easily into the howdah on the back of a caparisoned elephant, and those from the old royal stables still carry visitors up the winding road through seven gates to the spacious outer courtyard of this enchanting palace.

So exquisite were the carvings on the marble panels of the Hall of Public Audience, built by Jai Singh I, that they provoked the envy of the Emperor Jahangir, and the Rajput ruler prudently had all but a tiny portion covered with stucco.

Jai's father, Man Singh, Commander-in-Chief of Akbar's armies, constructed most of the existing buildings and a small temple to Kali, with an image brought by Man Singh from a campaign in Bengal, is still used by the former ruling family.

The exalted view from the back of a royal elephant as one rides up the long ramp to Amber, accompanied on foot by an itinerant musician playing the *ravanhatha* with its coconut-shell soundbox and bow with jingling bells, can transport the imaginative into the exotic past. Jai Singh's inner palace is reached through the elaborate Ganesh Pol, a massive, three-storey gateway covered with tempera paintings. The elephant-headed god, wearing a crown and robes, is seated over the entrance.

Delicately fretted marble grilles fill the windows of the upper galleries where, themselves hidden from view, the royal ladies could watch the spectacular arrival of their lord or visiting princes, gorgeously costumed, their jewelled aigrettes flashing from brilliant turbans.

The brooding fort of Jaigarh, higher up the hill, makes no bones about its function. Until very recently the fabled treasures of the Amber Kachchwahas were stored here in deep vaults, entered by each ruler only once in his lifetime, after his accession, when he was allowed to choose just a single item for his personal use.

Down in Sawai Jai Singh's new rose-pink city of Jaipur, his walled city palace is built in the typical Rajput style with fretted screens and fragile pillars supporting carved balconies, and still serves to house members of the ruling family. Rajmata Gayatri Devi (Ayesha to her friends), an internationally acknowledged beauty and widow of the last ruler, HH Sawai Man Singh II, was married from this palace and has many memories of the rambling building and its occupants.

It was in this palace that the Maharajas of Jaipur were installed, on the early-eighteenth-century *gadi*, a wooden frame covered with silver plate. Fans of yak-tails and peacock feathers are the symbols of state, held by attendants on formal occasions, while a golden howdah on display was used in 1961 by Queen Elizabeth of Great Britain and the late Maharaja. Surya, the Sun God, is shown flanked by two lions, and peacocks adorn the doors.

Close by, but outside the palace walls, is one of the most remarkable, original and much photographed of all Rajput palaces, the eighteenth-century Hawa Mahal or Palace of Winds. It is a five-storey, pyramid-shaped rose-pink façade with practically no depth. The strange structure, with its mass of semi-octagonal bays, carved sandstone grilles, finials and domes, was in fact a cool, airy grandstand from which the palace ladies could watch the life of the city and lively processions.

101 Amber Palace: a carved plaster window inset with coloured glass, and above it a mirrored ceiling

On the outskirts of Jaipur, in 1835, Maharaja Sawai Ram Singh II built a four-roomed pavilion for his governess, Kesar, who was also his mother's personal maid. Since the area abounded in big game, the villa soon became a hunting-lodge and over the years was gradually enlarged, becoming a royal guest-house, the wilder parkland around it transformed into formal gardens.

In 1925 Sawai Man Singh, an extremely shy young man, made it his private residence, where he could indulge in his favourite sport of polo without the ordeal of a daily public ride from the city palace. To watch Jai, as he was affectionately known, play a strenuous game of polo with a crack team of Rajput princes, then switch to bicycle polo with equal enthusiasm, was a special treat for his visitors. The palace was now called Rambagh after the builder of the original small villa, and had become a rambling, luxurious work of art, housing the Maharaja and his household.

In 1958 Jai saw the writing on the wall and he decided to turn Rambagh into an hotel. The family moved to the smaller eighteenth-century Raj Mahal, the remodelled former British Residency set in fifty-two acres of land, originally constructed as a summer residence for the royal harem, and now that too is an hotel.

Among the many Rajput palaces that have been turned into hotels are those of Bikaner and Jodhpur. The latter, the Umaid Bhawan, is a massive domed structure of reddish stone just outside the city, and was one of the largest private homes in the world. It took more than four thousand men sixteen years to build between 1929 and 1944 – it looks like a slightly smaller version of what was the Viceregal Lodge in Delhi, and is about as homely. In fact it was designed by the British architects responsible for the government buildings of the capital. Like Udaipur, Bikaner and Jaipur, Jodhpur too has its private swimming-pool, a vast indoor lake with marble pillars and murals. Huge marble halls and public rooms adorned with stuffed tigers and leopards, monumental staircases and a maze of corridors make this an impressive but far from traditional Rajput palace.

By contrast, the old palace in Jodhpur fort on the Hill of Strife is a mass of fretted pale pink or white stone, the columns and walls covered with a plaster of crushed cowrie shells polished to look exactly like marble. There is a grim air about the exterior of the fort. Could it be the memory of Maharaja Jodh's seventeen sons and fifty-two daughters, who are said to have been sacrificed in 1459 in the presence of their father, together with the architect of the fort, Bambhi Rajra, who was interred alive to ensure the protection of the gods – and the secret of its defences?

Jodhpur's five-coloured flag portrays a falcon, the form sometimes assumed by Durga, the patron goddess of the state. The throne is placed on a red velvet carpet while the state shields show both the sun and the moon symbols. The *gadi* with its peacock arm-rests and gilded elephants is of white marble, and was last used when the present representative of the royal family received his investiture at the age of four after his father was killed in a plane accident.

The Raika Bagh, which was the ruler's favourite residence when Kipling visited him, can be seen about a kilometre from the city proper. This was not a palace, for the lower floor was filled with horses in immaculate quarters, each animal with at least one groom, some with four. But neither was it a stable, for the upper floors were sumptuous royal apartments. The Maharaja loved his horses to such an extent that he wanted to live among the four hundred or more (with his stud farms he had over twelve hundred). None was ever put down, even if crippled. And whenever a horse died, it was wrapped in a white sheet strewn with flowers and borne by weeping grooms to the burial grounds. Today the Raika Bagh is used as government offices, no longer in a large estate but with a small green garden surrounding it.

Bikaner, the younger house of Jodhpur, carries three white hawks on its five-coloured flag, with the green tree commemorating the fact that Kala Mati, Bikaner's patron goddess, once turned the thorny jungle around the city into an orchard of fruit trees. And the story attached to Bikaner's motto, *Jai Jangal dar Badshah* ('Hail to the King of the Desert'), stems from the time when most of the Rajput states had become vassals of the Emperor Akbar, who sent the rulers and their armies abroad to fight his battles. Many of the princes objected to crossing the River Indus to serve in Afghanistan and asked Bikaner to be their spokesman, since his was the least accessible state for Akbar's anticipated vengeance. Bikaner agreed, on condition that the princes would in future greet him with the title of 'King of the Desert'.

The soft grey-pink stone fortress of Junagadh, with nearly forty pavilions, was begun by Raja Rai Singh in the sixteenth century and added to over the centuries. The Chintamani palace within the walls is of golden sandstone from Jaisalmer, chosen to please the Maharaja's bride, Rani Guna from that state. The sun and the moon, symbols of Bikaner and Jaisalmer, plus the lotus, emblem of Shiva, appear in the decoration of many of the rooms. Two enormous statues of elephants guard the main entrance, over which is a small *toran*, a model wooden gateway like a miniature portcullis, with an image of Ganesha sitting inside. Especially in Jaisalmer, even simple houses have a form of *toran* over the entrance. When a bridegroom arrives to claim his bride he is mounted on an elephant, if a prince, or if approaching smaller buildings, on a horse. The *toran* is lowered so that he can touch it with his sword and a green branch which he carries, indicating that he comes in peace but that if necessary he will use his sword to take his bride by force.

A silver throne with peacock arms stands in Bikaner's Karan Mahal palace, with its splendid painted gold and scarlet ceiling and walls, while in the Chhatra Mahal, a penthouse for the Maharani, open on all four sides to catch the breeze, the walls are covered with Delft and blue Chinese plates, with a frieze around the upper edges depicting a lively Krishna dancing with the *gopis*. The nineteenth-century red sandstone Lalgarh Palace is set in gardens on the outskirts of the city, and part of it has been converted into an hotel, run by the state itself and retaining the flavour of the leisurely nineteenth-century way of life. Family retainers wait by your door to answer the slightest whim and photographs of royal picnics and hunting parties hang on the walls. Adjoining it is the ruler's personal palace, the red sandstone intricately carved to represent wood. Live peacocks dance everywhere and in the vast entrance hall are busts of Queen Victoria and King Edward VII.

About thirty kilometres away at Gajner, once the private game reserve of the rulers and now a sanctuary, more peacocks dance on the lawns between the country palace (now an hotel) and the lake.

Then there is Jaisalmer, to which the late Maharaja of Bikaner, closely related by marriage, built his own private railway line. The sumptuous royal train can now be hired by parties relishing a taste of princely travel. The fortified city, begun in 1156 by Maharawal Jaisal, rises out of the flat desert like some gigantic island. Standing on the ramparts looking across the sandy waste, it is easy to imagine Marco Polo arriving with a caravan on his way to the lands of the Great Khan, and the Italian adventurer must have felt the same sense of wonder at this delicately fashioned, isolated city as does today's visitor.

On the Jaisalmer coat of arms a bird, representing the goddess Durga, sits upon a yellow shield with black *burjas* – crenellations of a desert fort. A bare left arm holds a broken spear, recalling the story that Jaisal was once struck by a horse with a magic spear. Desert antelopes sprinkled with gold coins support the shield, the coins being in recognition of Jaisalmer's dependence on the wealthy Jain banking community. The motto below is 'The Guardian of the Northern Gate of India'.

Just inside the main inner gateway, by the royal palace, is a white marble platform reached by a flight of steps leading to a marble throne. Here the ruler would sit in public audience during the Diwali Festival of Lights. Next to the platform is the well where Prince Jaisal met the hermit and saw the inscription prophesying the building of the castle.

In the Kali temple opposite, the Ashapuri horse-worship ceremonies were held, while in the royal complex itself are a number of exquisitely carved palaces, one leading to another in an intricate maze of corridors and open galleries. The old city is a place of private mansions, *havelis*, every one finely fashioned from the same golden stone. *Haveli*, a word of Persian origin, means an enclosed space, usually a residential block about five storeys high, surrounding an open court. Several families, usually related, inhabit the block, whose architectural design makes for natural air-conditioning.

In contrast are the eighteenth-century pleasure palaces of the Bharatpur rulers at Deeg, built of pale cream sandstone and white marble, set in large, formal Mughal gardens. Nur Jahan, the lovely Persian empress of Jahangir, once owned the marble swing on the terrace, while one of the enormous bedrooms contains the black marble bed on which the corpses of the emperors were laid.

The Deeg palaces, with their many unusual features and their perfection of detail, are regarded as some of the finest in Rajasthan. But there are far too many throughout Rajput territory to be described here. Alwar's forbidding fortified hilltop structures in a narrow, desolate gorge include the Salim Mahal, where Prince Salim, later to become Emperor Jahangir, lived in exile for three years. The romantic little Siliserh Lake Palace, now also a state hotel, was built by a young ruler who fell in love with a village girl whom he heard singing as he rode past her home. The prince leapt over the garden wall to woo the girl, whose brothers, returning unexpectedly, threatened to kill him. Revealing his identity, the prince promised to marry the maiden, and the Siliserh palace was built so that she might look over the lake to her old village home.

The majority of Rajasthan's princes and princesses today are serious men and women dedicated to their people's welfare, often representing their

102 Cenotaphs of the maharajas of Bikaner on the outskirts of the city

country overseas. Many have taken over the running of state hotels and administration. Lt-Colonel Bhawani Singh, son of the late Maharaja Sawai Man Singh of Jaipur, is one of the most active, managing the Raj Mahal Palace hotel. Incidentally, his marriage in 1965 to a princess of Sirmour was the last of the splendid regal Rajput weddings. After Partition, his father was appointed the first Rajpramukh (Governor) of the newly-integrated states of Rajasthan, and later became India's Ambassador to Spain. His widow, now Rajmata Gayatri Devi, in 1960 made a career for herself as a politician: she was elected as a Member of Parliament, and later became Director of the Rajasthan Tourist Board.

Another Rajput ruler elected to represent his people in Parliament was Karni Singh, son of the late Maharaja Sadul Singh, while in 1978 the former Maharaja of Jodhpur, Gaj Singh, went to the West Indies as India's High Commissioner. On the sudden death of his father, the Maharao Raja of Bundi, in December 1977, his son Ranji Singh left his job with the huge industrial Birla complex in Delhi to return to Bundi and carry out the duties of administering the state.

Maharana Bhagwat Singh of Mewar, whose title has some fourteen centuries of history behind it, qualified for the Indian Civil Service and was attached to the Guides Regiment on the North-West Frontier before Partition. Mewar rulers had always been conservative about foreign travel; in fact, Bhagwat Singh was the first member of his family to travel abroad, in 1960, and the next year he was host to two First Ladies, Her Majesty Queen Elizabeth and Mrs Jacqueline Kennedy.

When India gained her independence the Udaipur ruler voluntarily dropped his hereditary titles, which include *Hindu Surya* (The Indian Sun) and *Maharajdhiraj* (Great Prince of Princes), but Maharana is a family title and that alone was retained.

Meanwhile, an extremely devout man, he takes his traditional duties as Diwan or Prime Minister of Eklingji very seriously. Although the city palace had been given to the Government of India as a national monument, lack of funds and of interest was causing its gradual decay. When the property was returned to the ruler in 1969 he set up a charitable foundation with a generous donation for its upkeep as a national museum. Students' hostels and a public school were opened in 1974 in former palace buildings as well as a dispensary and a research library. Similar stories can be told of the other Rajput families who were once rulers of their states.

Not everyone can visit Rajasthan. But for those who can, it reveals a new dimension in both spiritual and physical experience.

Alas, my brother! Mighty Kings and Lords,
Proud princes, courtiers, loveliest maidens gay,
Bards and their tales of ancient chivalry,
Homage to Time! All these have passed away.
Bratvihara, Sataka

103 Sikar City Palace: a gilded and painted panel depicting the procession of Rao Raja Bhairon Singhji carried by an elephant

Glossary

Adinath: first of Jain *tirthankars* (saints)

Agni: god of fire

Agnikula: Rajputs claiming origin in the sacred firepit

Ahimsa: non-violence

Amba Mata: early fertility goddess

Ambika: earth deity

Amalaka: ornamental stone ring round *sikara* representing doorway to heaven

Ardha-Mandapa: portico of Hindu or Jain temple

Arthashastra: title of book on theory of political economy, by 4th-century BC politician Kautalya

Aryans: early semi-nomadic tribes from central Asia

Asha: Rajput alcoholic drink

Asvamedha: royal horse sacrifice, an ancient Rajput ceremony

Baoli: stepped well

Banya: Hindu or Jain merchant

Banyan tree: Ficus indica, large Indian fig-tree with aerial branch-roots, often regarded as sacred

Bhagavad Gita: 'Song of God', Krishna's poetic discourse, part of the Mahabharata epic

Bhairava or *Chaumunda:* Shiva's destructive aspect

Bhakti: devotion

Bharat Natyam: classic dance form

Bhat: traditional bard

Bhattis: Rajput clan claiming descent from the moon

Bhils: hill tribe, possibly descendants of Late Stone Age inhabitants of Rajasthan

Bhopa: minstrel

Bhudevi: earth goddess and Vishnu's second consort

Brahma: the Creator, first of the Hindu trinity

Brahmanas: appendices to Vedic texts on ritual and sacrifice

Brahmin: priestly caste, first of four Hindu castes

Chaitya: sacred enclosure; Buddhist place of worship

Chandravanshi: Rajputs claiming descent from the moon

Changi: royal insignia

Charan: traditional genealogist, bard

Chauhans: Rajputs claiming origin from the sacred firepit; Agnikula

Chaumurthi: four-faced statue

Chhatri: royal cenotaph in form of domed, open pavilion; lit. 'umbrella', symbol of royalty

Chishti: Dervish order brought to India from Khorassan, Iran, by the Muslim missionary Khwaja Moinuddin Chishti of Ajmer (1141–1226)

Dargah: mausoleum of Muslim saint

Darshan: 'viewing' of deity or holy personage

Dharma: Buddhist teaching; piety, spirit

Dharamshala: pilgrim hostel

Dhol: large, double-headed drum

Dhoti: ankle-length loin-cloth worn by men

Dhurri: cotton floor-covering

Digambara: Jain sect, lit. 'sky-clad', nude

Diwali: Hindu festival of lights, dedicated to goddess Lakshmi

Diwan-i-Am: hall of public audience

Diwan-i-Khas: hall of private audience

Domama: large drum, similar to kettle-drum

Durbar: court, audience given by royalty

Durga: consort of Lord Shiva, goddess Parvati in her warlike aspect

Dussehra: Hindu festival preceding Diwali, when Rajputs worship Durga

Ektara: one-stringed musical instrument

Fakir: religious mendicant

Gadi: throne

Gan: Shiva in his aspect as Gauri's consort

Ganesha: elephant-headed god of good fortune, patron of writers, son of Lord Shiva

Gangaur: spring festival celebrated by women

Garbha-griha: inner sanctuary of Hindu temple; lit. 'womb-house'

Garuda: heavenly vehicle of the deities, mythical bird

Gauri: the goddess Parvati worshipped at Gangaur as faithful, happy wife

Gavaksa: ray-eyed decorative temple motif

Ghaghara: full skirt worn by Rajput women

Ghat: shallow steps to lake or river, used for bathing and laundry

Ghi: clarified butter

Ghummar: circular folk-dance, performed by women

Gopi: milkmaid or daughter or wife of cowherd

Guhilot: founder of Mewar (Udaipur) dynasty

Hanuman: monkey god, beneficent, guardian spirit

Haveli: mansion, particularly in Jaisalmer

Holi: Hindu spring carnival, celebrated with coloured powders and water

Indra: god of thunder and rain and of the heavens

Jains: religious sect founded in 6th century BC

Jats: probably descendants of central Asian invaders, rulers of Bharatpur and Dholpur

Jauhar: deliberate battle to the death by Rajputs garbed in wedding finery, when defeat seems certain, after their women immolate themselves, leaving enemy with an empty victory

Karttikeya: god of war; Shiva's second son

Kachhwahas: ruling dynasty of Amber/Jaipur, claiming descent from the sun

Kachi Ghori: male folk-dance

Kajal (kohl): eye-black made from soot and oil

Kalawa: dyed thread decorating shrines

Kali: consort of Lord Shiva, fierce incarnation of Parvati as goddess of smallpox and disaster

Kalpa-vriksha: symbolic 'tree of life' bearing different fruits

Kancholi: backless bodice worn with *ghaghara* skirt

Kaputli: Rajasthani puppet theatre

Karwahad: large cauldron in which quantities of food are cooked for pilgrims attending religious festivals

Kathak: north Indian Rajput dance form

Kauravas: princes of ruling house in Mahabharata epic

Khandra: Rajput double-edged sword

Khayal: folk theatre

Kheer: sweet rice dish

Krishna: 8/7th-century BC chief of Yadava tribe, and incarnation of Lord Vishnu, the Preserver

Kshatriyas: Aryan warriors, second in rank among four Hindu castes

Kumkum or *sindura:* vermilion powder

Kurta: loose shirt for men and women

Lakshmi: goddess of wealth and beauty, consort of Vishnu

Langas: popular ballad singers

Lingam: phallic symbol associated with Shiva

Lingam-yoni: male/female symbols associated with Shiva and Parvati

Madrasseh: Muslim theological college

Mahabharata: world's longest epic poem, probably compiled between 4th century BC and 4th century AD

Mahal: palace, mansion, district

Mahavira: twenty-fourth and greatest of Jain *tirthankars*

Maharaja: title given to major princely rulers, lit. 'Great King'

Mandapa: pillared hall of temple

Mandan: hair-cutting ceremony

Marwar: lit. 'Land of the dead'. Desert, former kingdom of Rathore Rajputs of Jodhpur

Mehndi: henna paste decorating hands and feet

Mela: fair

Mewar: former kingdom of Sisodia Rajputs of Udaipur

Mihrab: prayer-niche in mosque, facing Mecca

Minar: minaret of mosque

Minas: jungle tribe of Rajasthan

Minbar: Muslim pulpit

Mor: peacock-feather coronet

Murti: unusually formed stones regarded as sacred

Nandi: sacred bull, vehicle of Shiva

Natya Shastra: ancient dance treatise

Nataraj: Shiva as Cosmic Dancer

Nazar: traditional formal tribute to a ruler

Odhni: veil or shawl worn by Rajput women

Paliya, Jujhar: lit. 'sacrificial pillar', memorial to warriors killed in battle, and to their *satis*

Pan: digestive mixture of lime, betel-nuts, cardamoms, etc., wrapped in betel leaves, chewed after meals

Pandavas: five brothers, heroes of Mahabharata epic

Parvati: goddess of the mountain and of beauty (see also Gauri, Kali, Durga)

Peepul: wild fig-tree, *Ficus religiosa,* regarded as sacred (also called Bo tree)

Phad: scroll-painting illustrating folk-stories

Pichwai: religious painting on cloth

Pindaris: mounted Rajput marauders of 17th to 19th centuries

Pinjrapol: Jain veterinary hospital

Pir: Muslim mystic

Prasad: food blessed by priests

Pugri or *safa:* turban

Puja: act of worship

Pujari: temple priest

Puranas: sacred Hindu texts composed *c.*1st millennium BC

Purdah: lit. 'curtain', seclusion of women

Qawwal: professional Muslim religious singer

Radha: beloved of Lord Krishna

Raga: melody based on limited number of notes

Rakhi: bracelet

Raksha Bandhan: bracelet ceremony in which women 'adopt' men as brothers to defend their honour

Rama: hero of Ramayana, one of Vishnu's incarnations

Ramayana: epic poem composed *c.*5th century BC dealing with events *c.*1500 BC

Rana, Maharana: hereditary title of Udaipur rulers

Rani, Maharani: queen, wife of ruler

Rao, Raoraja, Maharao Raja: hereditary titles of rulers of Kota and Bundi

Raslila: folk theatre based on Radha-Krishna romance

Rathores: Rajput family ruling Jodhpur

Ravanhatha: stringed musical instrument played with a bow

Rawal, Maharawal: lit. 'of the royal house', hereditary title of Jaisalmer rulers

Rig Veda: collection of early Aryan hymns

Sadhu: Hindu holy man

Sanga: community of Buddhist monks

Saraswati: goddess of arts, music and learning, consort of Brahma

Sati: lit. 'virtuous woman', state attained by widow mounting her husband's funeral pyre

Saptaswa: seven-headed horse (or seven horses) drawing Sun God's chariot

Shakti: female energy, creative force of universe

Shiva: the Destroyer, third of the Hindu trinity

Sikara: temple spire

Sindura: vermilion powder

Sisodias: later family name taken by Guhilot (Udaipur) ruling family

Sita: Prince Rama's consort in the Ramayana epic

Sohag: ritual suicide committed by wives whose husbands are living, but about to die

Srinathji: Lord Krishna

Stambha: monolithic pillar, tower

Sudras: fourth and lowest of Hindu castes; labourers, menial workers

Sufi: lit. 'wool', Muslim mystic, dervish, wearing garment of wool

Surya: sun god

Suryavanshi: Rajput clans claiming descent from the sun

Svetambara: yellow- or white-robed Jain sect

Swayamvara: ancient Hindu ceremony whereby a princess chose her own husband from a selected group

Tabla: hand drum

Tank: artificial lake

Teej: Hindu festival of swings

Terdh tali: acrobatic dance story of Ram Deoji

Tika, tilak, or *bindi:* red mark on forehead, symbol of royal investiture or religious ceremony, and of married Hindu women

Tirthankar: lit. 'perfect soul, ford-maker', Jain saint

Tonga: one-horse carriage

Torana: arched gateway to temple; miniature gateway placed over secular entrance to dwelling

Trigore: three-storeyed temple structure

Trimurthi: three-faced statue

Tulsi, tulasi: sacred basil plant

Upanishads: mystical Hindu religious texts, part of the Vedas

Urs: death anniversary of Muslim saint

Vanshavalis: keepers of genealogies

Varuna: god of wind

Vedas: sacred literature of ancient Aryans, oldest known written religious texts, probably composed between 1500 and 900 BC

Vaishyas: third of four Hindu castes, farmers and traders

Vihara: Buddhist monastery

Vina: stringed instrument

Vishnu: the Preserver, second in the Hindu trinity

Yoni: symbol of female principle

Zenana: women's apartments

Bibliography

AGRAWAL, R. C. 'Unpublished Temples of Rajasthan', *Arts Asiatiques* Vol. XL, 1965

AMBROSE, Kay *Classical Dances and Costumes of India*, Adam & Charles Black, London 1950

ANAND, Uma *Guide to Rajasthan*, India Tourism Development Corp., 1975

ARCHER, W.G. 'Rajasthan Painting, Kotah', MARG Vol. XI, March 1958

BASHAM, A. L. *The Wonder that was India*, Fontana, London 1971

BELLEW, Capt. *Views in India*, Published for the author, 1833

CAMERON, Roderick *Time of the Mango Flower*, Heinemann, London 1958

COOMARASWAMY, Ananda *Rajput Painting*, Oxford University Press, 1916

DAVAR, Satish 'Architecture', MARG Vol. XXX No. 4, Sept. 1977

DAVE, J. H. *Immortal India* Vol. II, Bharatiya Vidya Bhavan, Bombay 1959

DAVENPORT, Hugh *The Trials and Triumphs of the Mewar Kingdom, Udaipur*, Maharana Mewar Charitable Foundation, 1975

DEVI, Gayatri and Santha Rama Rau *A Princess Remembers*, Lippincott, Philadelphia 1976

DEVENISH, J. A. *The Bhawans or Garden Palaces of Dig, Bharatpur State*, Allahabad 1903

DHAMIJA, Jasleen *Indian Folk Arts and Crafts*, National Book Trust, India 1970

DHAMIJA, Jasleen 'The Pechwais of Nathdwara', Times of India Annual, 1965

EDWARDES, Michael *Raj*, Pan Books, London 1969

EDWARDES, Michael *Indian Temples and Palaces*, Paul Hamlyn, London 1969

FANE, Henry Edward *Five Years in India*, Henry Colburn, London 1852

FOSTER, W. (ed) *The Embassy of Sir Thomas Roe to India, 1615–19*, London 1926

GASCOIGNE, Bamber *The Great Moghuls*, Harper & Row, New York & London 1971

GOETZ, Hermann *The Art and Architecture of Bikaner*, Bruno Cassirer, Oxford 1950

GOETZ, Hermann 'The Nagaur School of Painting', *Artibus Asiae* XII, 1949

GOETZ, Hermann 'The First Golden Age of Udaipur', *Ars Orientalis*, II

GOLISH, Vitold de *Splendeur et Crépuscule des Maharajahs*, Hachette, Paris 1963

GUPTA, C. S. 'Fairs and Festivals', Census of India 1961: Vol. XIV, Rajasthan

GUPTA, Om Prakash *Mount Abu*, Sasta Sahitya Press, Ajmer 1960

HEBER, Bishop R. *Journey through the Upper Provinces of India*, Calcutta 1820

HOLMES, T. R. E. *History of the Indian Mutiny*, W. H. Allen, London 1888

HURLIMANN, Martin *India*, Thames & Hudson, London 1967

JACQUEMONT, Victor (trs Catherine A. Phillips) *Letters from India 1829–1832*, Macmillan & Co., London 1936

JAIN, C. R. *The Practical Dharma*, The Indian Press Ltd, 1929

JAYADEVA (12th cent. AD) (trs George Keyt) 'Gita Govinda', from *A Treasury of Asian Literature*, Mentor Books, 1956

JAYANTAVIJAYAJI, Muni Shri *Holy Abu*, Shri Yashovijaya Jaina Granthamala, 1954

KEAY, John *India Discovered*, Windward, 1981

KIPLING, John Lockwood *Beast and Man in India*, Macmillan & Co., London 1891

KIPLING, Rudyard *From Sea to Sea* Vol. I, Doubleday, Page & Co., New York 1907

KRAMRISCH, Stella *The Art of India through the Ages*, Phaidon Press, 1955

LANNOY, Richard *The Speaking Tree*, Oxford University Press, 1974

LOTHIAN, Sir Arthur Cunningham *Kingdoms of Yesterday*, John Murray, London 1951

MUNDY, Captain *Sketches in India* Vol. II, John Murray, London 1832

NOON, Sir Firozkhan *India*, Collins, London 1941

PANDEY, B. N. (ed) *A Book of India*, Collins/Rupa & Col, 1977

PAL, H. Bhisham *The Temples of Rajasthan*, Prakash, Alwar, Jaipur 1969

PIEPER, Jan 'Arboreal Art & Architecture in India', AARP Vol. 12, Dec. 1977

PRABHAVANANDA, Swami, & Christopher Isherwood (trs) *Bhagavad-Gita*, Phoenix House, London 1948

PRABHAVANANDA, Swami & Frederick Manchester (trs) *Upanishads*, Vedanta Soc. of Southern California with Mentor Books, 1957

RAU, Santha Rama *This is India*, Harper, New York 1954

ROWLAND, Benjamin *The Art and Architecture of India*, Penguin Books, 1967

SEN, K. M. *Hinduism*, Pelican Books, 1961

SHARMA, Dr Y. D. 'Kalibangan: Indus Valley Civilisation', Times of India Annual, 1965

SOLOMON, W. E. Gladstone *Masterpieces of Mogul Art*, Oxford University Press, 1932

SPEAR, Percival *A History of India* Vol. II, Pelican, 1965

TADDEI, Maurizio *The Ancient Civilisations of India*, Nagel n.d.

TERRY, Edward *A Voyage to East India*, 2nd ed., London 1777

THAPUR, Romila *A History of India* Vol. I, Pelican, 1966

THOMAS, P. *Epics, Myths and Legends of India*, D. B. Taraporevala Sons & Co., Bombay n.d.

TIME- LIFE INTERNATIONAL *The Epic of Man*, 1962

TOD, Col. James *Annals and Antiquities of Rajasthan*, Oxford University Press, 1920

WATSON, Major John W. 'Rajputana', Indian Antiquary, Bombay, August 1873

WHEELER, Sir Mortimer *Early India and Pakistan*, D. B. Taraporevala Sons & Co., Bombay 1959

Acknowledgements

To the people of Rajasthan themselves I owe my most profound gratitude. Many friends were made along the way, but it was thanks to the generous encouragement of Dr Karan Singh, the former Maharaja of Kashmir, then Minister of Tourism, that I was invited to create a book on India and later this book on Rajasthan. One great privilege was to travel with Gayatri Devi, former Maharani of Jaipur, to many remote villages in her State and to meet her people. The former Maharaja of Bharatpur gave us unrivalled hospitality in his palace, and also guided us to the fortress on the Rup Lake at Deeg and his private wild-life reserve at Ghana. Carol George, wife of the Canadian High Commissioner to India, was frequently our companion on the road, and always in spirit. Her tireless and educated research made an invaluable contribution to the realization of this book. In my Rome studio, Sally Marcucci, Franco Bugionovi and Antonella Carini were responsible for interpreting my wishes.

A mystic chain of events led to many years of creative collaboration with Mitchell Crites, not only in Rajasthan but throughout India. In Rajasthan we travelled in a state of wonder before the sacred and the profane. The colours of Rajasthan, the gilded idols, the carved marble temples and the 'palaces in the sand' made each day an event in the 'land of kings'.

ROLOFF BENY

Recent travels in Rajasthan refreshing old memories and gathering new material were arranged with the cooperation and active help of officials in various Government of India Tourist Departments in Delhi and Rajasthan. But it was the warm hospitality and affection spontaneously given over the years by many Rajput friends of long standing that instilled my deep love and admiration for the land of the dancing peacock and made possible the concept and creation of this long-planned tribute, which is for all of them.

SYLVIA A. MATHESON

Index

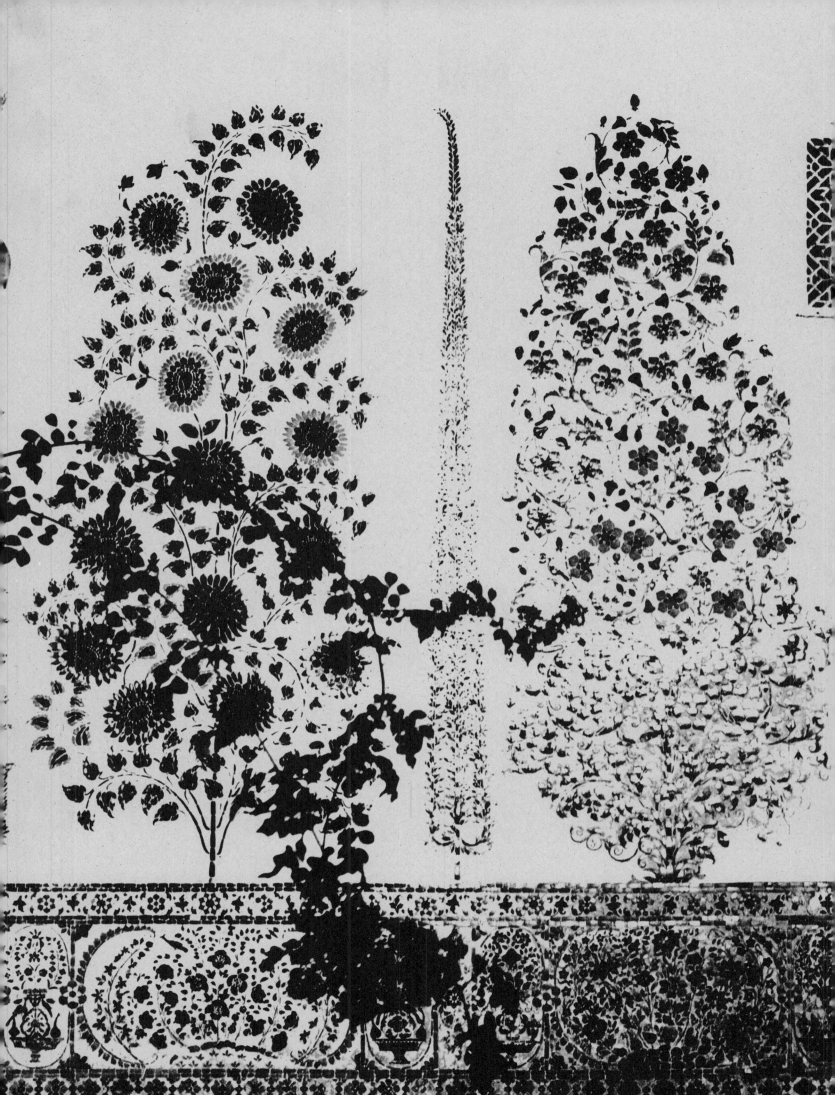